COMMITMENT

COMMITMENT

VAUGHN J. FEATHERSTONE

Bookcraft
Salt Lake City, Utah

Library of Congress Catalog Card Number 82-70249
ISBN 0-88494-453-0

3 4 5 6 7 8 9 10   89 88 87 86 85 84 83

Lithographed in the United States of America
PUBLISHERS PRESS
Salt Lake City, Utah

Contents

The Go-Getter

Commitment is a quality that combines determination with an intelligent goal. It is a great concentration or focus on something that requires labor to acquire or to reach. Of course, there is such a thing as weak commitment. That isn't what I am talking about. In fact, somehow to me, *weak* and *commitment* are not compatible words. By its very nature, *commitment* is a word that exudes strength. But it is not a declaration only: It has to include action. Thus, Joshua made the declaration of commitment to Jehovah in these words:

> Now therefore fear the Lord, and serve him in sincerity and in truth: and put away the gods which your fathers served on the other side of the flood, and in Egypt; and serve ye the Lord.
> And if it seem evil unto you to serve the Lord, choose you this day whom ye will serve; whether the gods which your fathers served that were on the other side of the flood, or the gods of the Amorites, in whose land ye dwell: but as for me and my house, we will serve the Lord. [Actually, the Hebrew text says *Jehovah*, not *the Lord*.] (Joshua 24:14-15.)

But when we look for a great commitment to Jehovah, we often turn to the young shepherd David, who went to the battlefront with his family's rations for the sons of Jesse who were serving in the army of Saul. To his astonishment he found that the Israelite host was stymied by a lone Philistine, a huge one, true; but, nevertheless, a mortal man. Not only that, but this Goliath was a heathen whose heart had not been broken and encircled by the bands of God's love. And his body did not carry the mark of the covenant. He was outside of the protection that David presumed all Israel enjoyed. In the purity and innocence of youth he had chosen whom he would serve. And it was not the gods of the Amorites nor of the Philistines. It was the Almighty who would never fail though all others may flee. No Goliath was a match for one Israelite and this God to whom David was committed in his youth with all his heart and all his mind.

So David shamed all Israel by marching out alone to face what everyone else presumed was certain death. His armor was the virtue bestowed by grace. His weapon was single-minded commitment. And his strength and skill were the strength and skill of Jehovah, who guided the stone that slew Goliath.

But David had prepared himself. His mind was schooled by the things he believed and refused to deny. His arm was strengthened by wielding the staff and the sling constantly in the protection of the family flocks. And his courage was steeled by facing and conquering the lion and the bear in hand to claw combat. Preparation is a part of commitment, too.

So commitment is a path. The first step is to say or write the commitment. May it be a noble one. The second is to prepare, including, perhaps, listing the obstacles that may turn you aside so that you can avoid them or prepare to climb over them. The third step is the action part, the time when you slay the "Goliath," or the dragon.

It will be hard to live a committed life if we are constantly aware of all the burdens of a lifetime, past and future. Because of the Atonement, we can drop the past and go forward step by step. Someone has said that "life by the inch is a cinch, but by the yard it is hard." It isn't the dramatic leaps that bring us up to

the summit of some Everest. It is the plodding, the forever putting of one foot in front of the other in the right direction that
gradually conquers the high mountain. Also, one must not make
the mistake of thinking he must be a David or she must be a
Joan of Arc. Usually the greater the planning, the smaller the
heroics. But we do have to have our minds made up not to shirk
work and to face danger if necessary in the fulfillment of our
commitments. No matter how well we plan, something unex-
pected will come along that will test our commitment. In such
cases the truly committed will keep going or get going while the
uncommitted will sit down and hope to find an easier path.

In 1921 Peter B. Kyne wrote *The Go-Getter, a Story That Tells
You How to Be One.* This book tells how Mr. Ricks, the owner of
a lumber and logging company, was having a problem with his
Shanghai office. His supervisor's explanation was that he was
surrounded by men who were too young for responsibility. In
addition, three managers had "gone rotten." The company
would be in trouble if things persisted as they were. About this
time a crippled veteran by the name of William E. Peck requested an interview for employment.

"Please give me a job. I don't care a hoot what it is, provided
I can do it. If I can do it, I will do it better than it has ever been
done before. If I can't do it, I will quit and save you the embarrassment of firing me."

The old man was impressed and, going over the heads of all
the executives and supervisors, hired William E. Peck. Bill was
warned to produce and not get out of line. "The first time you
tip a foul, you'll be warned. The second time, you'll get a month
lay-off to think about it. The third time you will be out for
keeps."

Peck was given the task of selling a lot of undesirable lumber
that the company was stuck with. He was happy. He said, "I can
sell anything at a fair price." He hit the ball hard. For two
months they saw nothing of him. He sold several boxcar loads
of skunk spruce, siding, shingles, Douglas fir, and redwood. He
sent orders back to the office almost daily. He sold five new

accounts and increased sales dramatically. So impressed was the owner that he thought Bill might be a good man to head up the Shanghai office. But, before a final decision, Bill would have to go through the "test."

The "test" was to send Bill on an errand to obtain a very expensive blue vase which had been described to him in detail. Bill was told to obtain it and deliver it to a stateroom in car seven on the train for Santa Barbara so that Mr. Ricks could take it to his wife for their anniversary. Bill was told the approximate location of the neighborhood — which street, which store, and the window where it could be seen. It was Sunday and after 3:00 P.M. when Bill went to find the vase. He went to the area where the vase had been seen but he searched in vain, street after street — two blocks of additional searching in all four directions, four more blocks before he finally discovered the object of his search. He kicked the door, making an infernal racket, but no one responded. He backed away and read the sign over the door, B. Cohen's Art Shop.

He limped to a hotel, picked up the phone book, and found nineteen B. Cohens. He searched for the art dealer in vain and then dialed all nineteen numbers. He emerged from the phone booth wringing wet from perspiration. It was 6:00 P.M., and his bad leg was starting to give out on him. Then he had a flash of thought, *Could the name have been spelled differently?* Was it Cohen, Cohan, Cohn, Kohn, or Coen? He went back to the art shop: It was spelled Cohn's Art Shop. He went back to the phone booth and began calling all the Cohns. On the sixth call he was lucky and got the right B. Cohn. The cook who answered the phone said that Mr. Cohn was dining at the house of a Mr. Simons in Mill Valley. There were three Mr. Simons, and Bill called all of them before connecting with the right one. Yes, Mr. Cohn was there, but who wished to speak to him? Mr. Heck? Mr. Lake? A silence followed, then the maid returned, "Mr. Cohn doesn't know any Mr. Lakes and wants to know the nature of the business."

"Tell him Mr. Peck wants to speak to him regarding a matter of grave importance." After a frustrating dialogue, Mr. Cohn came to the phone. Bill told him that he had to have the vase by 7:45 P.M. that night and he needed Mr. Cohn to come back across the Bay, open his store, and sell him the vase.

Bill was told to contact Mr. Joost. Again, Bill encountered the same kind of runaround as he tried to find Joost at one of several country clubs. He could not find Joost.

He borrowed a hammer then hailed a taxi. He was going back to the art store to break the window. But when he reached the shop, there was a policeman standing in front of the store. He left and came back and noticed the sign over the store read B. Cohen's Art Store. He sat down on a fire hydrant and cursed with rage. His weak leg hurt, the stump on his left arm developed a feeling that his missing hand itched. He took the taxi back to the hotel. Hope springing eternally in his breast, he called Mr. Joost, who then after their conversation had to verify with Mr. Cohn the entire story. If Mr. Kek would just wait at the art store, he would come over if the story was accurate.

At 9:15 P.M. Herman Joost arrived and brought the policeman along with him for protection, just in case. He opened and retrieved lovingly the blue vase; the cost was two thousand dollars. Bill had ten dollars, and Mr. Joost refused a check. Bill called Mr. Skinner from the company and asked to have two thousand dollars sent down. There was a time lock on the safe and no way to get the money. He tried Mr. Ricks's residence to see if he had the money. He had left for Santa Barbara. He tried everything. Finally he went back to his hotel, got his diamond ring with sapphires set in platinum. It was worth about twenty-five hundred dollars. He left it until he could bring the money.

It was too late to catch the train that left at 8:45 P.M. He went to the flying field at Mariner. He got the address of the pilot and awakened him at midnight. They headed south in the moonlight with the vase. An hour and a half later they landed in a field of stubble in the Salinas Valley. He limped to the railroad track; and when the train came he made a torch, stood between the tracks, and flagged down the train. The train slid to a halt, and the brakeman railed on Bill Peck violently. Bill climbed on board and said he would purchase a ticket. The brakeman said, "That's right, take advantage of your half-portion arm and abuse me. Are you looking for that little old man with the Henry Clay collar and the white muttonchop whiskers?"

"I certainly am."

"Well, he was looking for you just before we left San Francisco. He asked me if I had seen a one-armed man with a box under his good arm. I'll lead you to him."

A prolonged ringing at Mr. Ricks's stateroom door brought the old gentleman to the entrance in his nightshirt.

"Very sorry to have to disturb you, Mr. Ricks," said Bill, "but the fact is there were so many Cohens and Cohns and Cohans and it was such a job to dig up two thousand dollars that I failed to connect with you at 7:45 last night as ordered. It was absolutely impossible for me to accomplish this task in the time limit set; but I was resolved that you would not be disappointed. Here is the vase. The shop wasn't within four blocks of where you thought it was, sir; but I'm sure I found the right vase. It ought to be. It cost enough and was hard enought to get. So it should be a precious gift for your wife or anyone else."

Mr. Ricks stared at Bill Peck as if he were looking at a spook. "By all that's wonderful!" he murmured. "We changed the sign on you, we stacked the Cohens on you, and we set a policeman to guard the shop to keep you from breaking the window. We made you dig up two thousand dollars on a Sunday night in a town where you are practically unknown; and, while you missed the 8:00 P.M. train, you overtook it at 2:00 A.M. in the morning and delivered the vase. Come in and rest your poor old game leg, Bill. Brakeman, I am much obliged to you."

Bill Peck entered and slumped wearily down on the settee.

"So it was a plan?" he croaked, and his voice trembled with rage. "Well, sir, you're an old man, and you've been good to me; so I do not begrudge you your little joke. But, Mr. Ricks, I can't stand things like I could before I was crippled in the war. My leg hurts and my stump hurts and my heart hurts."

He paused, choking, and the tears of impotent rage filled his eyes.

"You shouldn't treat me that way, sir," he complained presently. "I've been trained not to question orders, even when they seem utterly foolish to me. I've been trained to obey them — on time, if possible; but, if impossible, to obey them anyhow. I've been taught loyalty to my chief, and I'm sorry my chief found it necessary to make a buffoon of me. I haven't had a very good time the past three years, and you can pa-pa-pass your skunk wood and larch rustic and short, odd-length stock to some slacker."

At this point Mr. Ricks apologized profusely and let Bill know that he had passed a test that only one other out of fifteen had passed and that the reward was a very highly paid position as the manager of the Shanghai office. By the time Mr. Ricks was through with his apology, Bill Peck had forgotten his rage; but the tears of his recent fury still glistened in his bold blue eyes. "Thank you, sir. I forgive you, and I'll make good in Shanghai."

"I know you will, Bill. Now tell me, son, weren't you tempted to quit when you discovered the almost insuperable obstacles I had placed in your way?"

"Yes, sir, I was. I wanted to commit suicide before I had finished telephoning all the Cohens in the world. And when I started on the Cohns, well, it was this way, sir. I just couldn't quit because that would have been disloyal to a man I once knew."

"Who was he?" Cappy Ricks demanded, and there was awe in his voice.

"He was my brigadier, and he had a brigade motto: It shall be done. When the divisional commander called him and told him to move forward with his brigade and occupy certain territory, our brigadier would say: 'Very well, sir. It shall be done.' If any officer in his brigade showed signs of shirking his job be-

cause it appeared impossible, the brigadier would just look at
him once. And then that officer would remember the motto and
go and do his job or die trying.

"The brigadier once sent for me and ordered me to go out
and get a certain German sniper. I'd been pretty lucky—some
days. He opened a map and said to me: 'Here's about where he
holes up. Go get him, Private Peck.'

"Well, Mr. Ricks, I snapped to it and gave him a rifle salute
and said, 'Sir, it shall be done.' I'll never forget the look that man
gave me.

"He came down to the hospital to see me after I'd walked
into one of the dustricair 88s. I knew my left wing was a total
loss, and I suspected my left leg was about to leave me, and I
was downhearted and wanted to die.

"He came and bucked me up. He said, 'Why, Private Peck,
you aren't half dead. In civilian life you're going to be worth a
half a dozen live ones, aren't you?' But I was pretty far gone, and
I told him I didn't believe it; so he gave me a hard look and said,
'Private Peck will do his utmost to recover, and as a starter he
will smile.'

"Of course, putting it in the form of an order, I had to give
him the usual reply as I grinned and said, 'Sir, it shall be done.'

"He was quite a man, sir, and his brigade had a soul—his
soul."

As William Peck told Mr. Ricks the name of the brigadier,
Ricks was visibly startled and said, "The brigadier was a candi-
date for an important job in my employ, and I gave him the test
of the blue vase." Then he explained how the brigadier succeeded in getting the vase.

Go-getters produce go-getters.

I would like to see *The Go-Getter,* by Peter B. Kyne, resurrected and reprinted. What a dramatic story about commitment!
There are a lot of other long-since-forgotten books that extolled
self-reliance and were not ashamed of the success ethic. Just
imagine what the Lord could do if all the members of the
Church when asked to do anything would answer as Bill Peck

did, "It shall be done," and then follow President Spencer W. Kimball's motto and "Do it."

Through the training of his brigadier and because of the stuff he was made of, Bill Peck made up his mind somewhere along the line that he would never remain defeated. From the time he made that decision, that commitment if you will, he was destined to succeed. All he needed was to get his feet on the path. In his case success was making money and overcoming obstacles. But it doesn't have to be money. It can be many things. In the case of a true Latter-day Saint it *will* be many things. We have a vision of a fully rounded life with success as the ultimate goal in all parts of the circle.

A member of a missionary committee showed us a visual aid that he called something like "A Faith Progression Chart." The first step he called "knowledge in the form of true information." The second step he called "decision to believe." The third he called "active faith or works." The last step he called "knowledge as testimony." The knowledge in this fourth step was the same as the knowledge in the first step. Only now it had a new dimension because it had been tried and proven true.

I would like to add a word each to steps one and two. The word I would add to step one is *vision.* When we have heard the truth about some righteous principle, whether it be temporal or spiritual, that is not enough. I repeat, just hearing the words is not enough. Even understanding the words in a hypothetical way is not enough. We need also to have the vision to see the value of that principle in our lives. It is not enough to see the value of the principle in the lives of others or in people's lives in general. We need also to see the value in our lives. We need to picture ourselves reaping the rewards of obedience to that principle. We need to see ourselves succeeding with it.

The word I would add to step two is *commitment.* Somehow commitment carries more force than decision. Of course, you can call these two words synonyms. But, as we have come to use them in our day, commitment seems to carry more of the get-up-and-keep-going meaning.

Perhaps I can illustrate this with a couple of stories.

I know a pretty good man who decided long ago to be true to the Church and to do certain other things. (What I have to say about him came from his own lips; so don't blame me if I sound too hard on him.) This man had great potential. It would be hard to find his equal in academic achievement or knowledge of the gospel. And the Lord blessed him with many marvelous spiritual experiences so that his testimony was immovable. Yet he never became a great servant of the Lord and essentially failed in most material things.

The problem was commitment, not decision. He had decided to be true to the gospel and to the Church. And he was. He did few, if any, negative things. But he was not committed to a plan of action. His family activities were not well planned, if planned at all. So the time would arrive and the activity would be a flop instead of an event. He hoped he'd get to the welfare farm; but he didn't actually schedule it and plan to be there. His home teaching visits were generally made; but they were last-minute desperate attempts to get something done since it was too late to do it right. And his business life was a mirror image of his Church life—as is so often the case. Somehow he never came to grips with the *now*. He was always living in the *future* or the *past* and letting the *present* run him instead of him running it. His life was reminiscent of that great insight from James: "A double minded man is unstable in all his ways." (James 1:8.) I don't know what will ever become of him. Because there are bright spots here and there on the record, I pray for the best. But his life could have been so different if he had been totally committed like the next man I want to tell you about.

I met this second man a year or two after I got married. He had a profound effect on my life; so I have to tell some personal background. I grew up in a basically LDS area; but we were not completely in the Church to begin with. My mother leaned toward the Catholic Church, but was not a member. There were seven children. Much of the time my mother had the double tasks of breadwinning and mothering. She worked nights and mothered in the daytime and slept when she could.

We all learned to help. I took my turn supporting the family. Then after high school and finding the right girl to take to the temple, I went to my mother and asked her permission to take my last two weeks' wages and get married, leaving the burden of the family on the next brother under me.

A year or two after we got married, my wife and I moved into the Hillside Stake and I met a great Latter-day Saint who was quite wealthy. I realize that some people think you can't be both great and wealthy, but I don't agree with that. Neither would they if they properly comprehended the scriptures and the lives of many wealthy Saints. A careful study of the lives of Brigham Young and Job alone should straighten out a lot of this kind of thinking. Of course, there are bad rich men. There also are bad poor men. The man I am telling about was a good rich man. He could have divested himself of all his money and property, but then his charities and some of his service would have been cut off and he would not have been an inspiration to a young man like me. I would not have seen a "vision" of what I could become.

This particular rich man has done a great deal of missionary work and has contributed lands and properties and many material things to the Church. I am sure that only he knows the extent of his charities. He had just been called as a stake missionary when I met him. He was also on the stake high council. I didn't understand why they would leave him in both callings. What they were doing, as I learned later, was preparing him for a calling as a mission president.

I was assigned as his companion. We had a district meeting at his residence. I remember walking into his home and being almost overcome by its beauty and comfort. I never had seen anything like that before in my life. I had been in some fairly nice homes, but not like his. My feet sank into the deep, thick carpeting. It was just a beautiful place with a handsome grand piano, big overstuffed chairs, a huge fireplace, and lovely paintings on the walls. I remember just going in and looking at all those things.

This was the middle of the winter, and as I began to take of

my overcoat, I found my host taking it off for me. I had never had anyone help me take off my overcoat before in my whole life. And this was not much of an overcoat. Someone had given it to me, and I had worn it for a few years. I was grateful to have it. I had known what it was to go without an overcoat. When I was at South High School I was in the a cappella choir, and we would sing all over Salt Lake City at Christmastime. I remember singing outside on a little plaza in Sugarhouse without an overcoat. All I had was a jacket someone had given me. There was about six inches of snow. It was still snowing, and the wind was blowing. I was embarrassed because people would say, "Aren't you cold?" And I'd say, "No, I feel just great!" I was really chilled to the bone, but I didn't want to let anyone know.

Anyway, I did wear my old overcoat to the stake missionary meeting, and my rich companion helped take it off. Then we went into the living room. I didn't hear much that night. I just looked around and thought about what my companion had accomplished in a temporal way and what that had enabled him to do in a spiritual way.

I remember I gave the closing prayer after we had finished our business. Then I went over to the closet and discovered that my coat was gone. Frankly, the thought went through my mind that my host had thrown it away. I decided I wouldn't ask for it. Then all of a sudden he was standing behind me, holding my coat for me to put it on. I had never had anyone do that before. I put my arm in and it went between the lining and the sleeve and got caught down there. If it had been possible, I'd have made a hole so my hand could have come out. I couldn't quite do that, so I had to pull my arm back out all the way and try to get it in the right place. It was very embarrassing.

I was never the same after that night. As I was walking home I knew all of a sudden that I could be something better and do something bigger. I had seen that my companion not only had all those fine material possessions, but his life was committed to the Lord's service. I decided I wanted to be that kind of a man. I used him as an example for a long time; and as I have gone

around the Church, I have found that there are many like him who are worthy of emulation. They have a common characteristic: They are committed. That is, they believe so strongly in what they are doing that they get it done. They are *go-getters.*

Solomon, in Ecclesiastes 9:10, sums up well the attitude of the go-getter. "Whatsoever thy hand findeth to do, do it with thy might." Do it. Do it with your might. That's commitment.

2

To Walk in High Places

As a new twelve-year-old Scout I attended a court of honor in which an older fellow in the troop, Jim Rasband, was awarded a beautiful red heart-shaped medal. It was called the Life Scout award. I remember how impressed we troop members were when it was pinned on his Scout shirt. That one experience of seeing an unusual Scout lift his head above the average boy and walk in high places probably contributed to my attainment of the Eagle rank.

I watched an older brother and other achievers excel and play football before large crowds of enthusiastic high school students. I saw young people succeed in speech, drama, student government, music, dance, and ROTC. Those who put forth sufficient effort and time usually became the best. Many years ago at Yale University the swim team was breaking many world records. A writer asked the coach how they were doing it. The coach replied, "I have taught them to break the pain barrier."

I attended Church not because I was forced to but because I desperately needed and wanted to. I saw men who walked in high places who were pure, gentle, kind. I met men who had time to spend with boys. Great men such as Percy Scofield,

Lincoln Parker, Don Stout, Bruford Reynolds. I remember Percy Scofield, our bishop, hiking into Dog Lake with us. He wasn't a young man, and the hike just about killed him; but he went with us.

During World War II Don Stout wrote to me from Europe. A tank had turned upside down in a pond, and he and his comrades were inside for several hours not knowing if they were going to drown or suffocate. He shared some of his experiences and then in the last paragraph he said, "Vaughn, I want you to know I have never had a beer or a cigarette, never a drink of liquor or tea. I have never had coffee or even a cola drink in spite of all the pressure from the boys in my company." I told that to a friend and he said it was impossible, that no man could do that. I answered, "If Don said he did it, he did it."

I was twelve when I read his letter. I wept as I thought about him, and I decided right then and there that I was going to walk in high places like Don Stout.

As I grew older, the men who impressed me the most were those who were involved in serving others. They were in bishoprics and in other ward and stake executive positions. They served as Scoutmasters and Aaronic Priesthood advisers. They were great fathers and caring home teachers. I made the decision that I wanted to serve. I wanted to be like them. They seemed to radiate happiness, and they were successful because they were content to serve.

Wilford Kimball was our bishop when I was an older teenager. He had two daughters in my age group, Ardyth and Virginia. Every, I mean *every*, Sunday evening we would go to Bishop Kimball's house. Always they would be there. Always we would have refreshments. Never once did any of us feel unwelcome. It wasn't just for a few months but literally for a few years. I don't know how they ever afforded it, let alone put up with ten to fifteen teenagers for two to three hours every Sunday night.

Of course, I don't mean to imply that a bishop and his wife who don't do this much are failing in their duty. I simply am calling attention to one great bishop and his wife who did it this way. They were well paid for their sacrifice. From that little group has come five or six bishops, several high councilors, two stake presidents, several counselors in stake presidencies, and wives of these priesthood brethren, not to mention the Church leadership these ladies supplied. Bishop Kimball himself was later called as a stake president and then as a mission president. Some others who were there became mission presidents. What a privilege to walk with Wilford Kimball and his wife in a high place, their home.

I made the decision that I wanted to walk in high places—not in an aspiring way, but I wanted to serve. It appeared to me that leaders did most of the serving.

When I was about eighteen, I heard of solemn assemblies and priesthood leadership meetings held in conjunction with stake conferences. I heard about nine-hour testimony meetings in the mission field. I heard about meetings in the assembly room in the temple, and I longed to be worthy to one day attend such meetings. I didn't ever want anything to come into my life that would prevent me from having such opportunities.

All of my life I have wanted to walk in high places, and I have. Some of the highest places in which I have walked have been the humble homes of our sweet Lamanite brethren. I have found high places in the service of our snowy-crowned, long-living friends in and out of the Church. I have found a high place with a new convert who was talking to a young man. The convert said, "Your father is a good old boy." Then he asked, "Do you know what a good old boy is?" The young man said no. The convert explained: "In Texas we have men who are great men, gentlemen—refined, dignified, fine men. The good old boy is one level higher." I have known some good old boys and walked in high places with them.

Those high places can show up in some unlikely places, too, as the following verse indicates:

> We have the nicest garbage man.
> He empties out our garbage can.

> He's just as nice as he can be.
>> He always stops and talks with me.
> My mother doesn't like his smell,
>> But, then, she doesn't know him well.

Perhaps this sweet verse expresses a sentiment that is not so surprising after all. The front page of the December 27, 1981, *Salt Lake Tribune* reported the results of a study by a state college in Pennsylvania which indicated that family members and neighbors hold garbage collectors in higher esteem than they do college professors. When we take time to really know people, we find much that is great and good about them. We are not so critical of failures or appearances. We begin to judge them for their true worth. Missionaries, for example, come to love those whom they serve simply because they serve them.

To all the men and women, old and young, to boyhood friends, to a great mom, to great brothers and sisters, to a wonderful wife, and to children with whom I have walked in high places, I say:

> There's a comforting thought at the close of the day,
> When I'm weary and lonely and sad,
> That sort of grips hold of my crusty old heart
> And bids it be merry and glad.
> It gets in my soul and it drives out the blues,
> And finally thrills through and through.
> It is just a sweet memory that chants the refrain:
> "I'm glad I touch shoulders with you!"
> Did you know you were brave, did you know you were strong?
> Did you know there was one leaning hard?
> Did you know that I waited and listened and prayed,
> And was cheered by your simplest word?
> Did you know that I longed for the smile on your face,
> For the sound of your voice ringing true?
> Did you know that I grew stronger and better because
> I had merely touched shoulders with you?
> I am glad that I live, that I battle and strive
> For the place that I know I must fill;
> I am thankful for sorrows. I'll meet with a grin
> What fortunes may send, good or ill.

> I may not have wealth, I may not be great,
> But I know I shall always be true.
> For I have in my life that courage you gave
> When once I rubbed shoulders with you.
>
> *—Unknown*

If you want to walk in high places, be prepared to make some sacrifices. Courage, integrity, purity, and spirituality will enable you to walk with great men, even leaders and rulers of nations, great business executives, and men of great wealth, without being afraid of feeling out of place. You can walk in the presence of bishops, stake presidents, General Authorities, and our prophet and be humbled but not fearful.

We now come to the commitments that must be made if we are to enjoy that most desirable of all successes, serving the Lord and his children. This success comes to those who heed the counsel of the General Authorities of this Church. Through obedience to the same commitments these men have generally become eminently successful in the business world, in their Church callings, and in their families. I suggest that you have the courage, wisdom, and good sense to follow their counsel. If you do, you always will walk in high places no matter what your specific callings may be.

Following their counsel represents commitment to a Christian standard. As we sow, so shall we reap. High standards reap high rewards: business success, trusted callings in the Church, and respect from decent people. Of course, we all suffer setbacks and temporary periods of seeming disillusionment when it seems that the rules do not work for us. Those are the times to remember the lesson of Job. He knew that he had lived according to the rules, so he did not make the mistake of blaming himself for his misfortunes. He kept his conviction that he was worthy. When it was all over, he realized that the Lord had tested him for a purpose, and his final reward exceeded all possible anticipation. So don't become discouraged and give up on yourself, on the rules, or on the gracious and merciful Creator.

Let me list and discuss some of the standards that Latter-day Saint priesthood leaders want you to consider. I will call them commitments, because you need to make commitments about these standards if you are to have the freedom and happiness that comes from walking in high places.

Good grooming is the first principle I would like to discuss. How a person grooms and dresses tells us much about what that person thinks of himself. There even have been times when custom or law prescribed the dress of trades, professions, and social classes. Some of this has carried over into our time and is used to reveal what people think about what they do or about their station in life.

Why do we send our missionaries forth clothed and groomed to reflect neatness, cleanliness, and discipline? Isn't it because we desire to make a good initial impression on those we meet so that our conduct and grooming will not stand in the way of generating an interest in the gospel? When you think of a great business executive, a prominent governmental official, a bishop or stake president, a ward or stake Relief Society president, what comes to mind? Generally it is a mental image of a well-groomed individual.

The way I dress has been determined by a desire not to offend people I love and respect. Many years ago, as a young man in my early twenties, I thought my way through this matter of hair cuts. In doing so, I considered the people with whom I wanted most to be associated. I decided that I didn't need to satisfy any whim by wearing a radical or unusual hair style. I decided to stay with a hair style that would give me an appearance of greater maturity and a "settled-down" look. From my earliest married days I have been deeply involved in heavy assignments in the Church. And because I really wanted to serve in the Kingdom, I was certainly not going to let an exterior image cause my priesthood leaders not to consider me for a call. It was not their prejudices I feared; because I know they usually do not have any. It was the realization that we need to put our best foot forward. It was the people who still need a lot of help whom I did not want to needlessly offend. The master fisherman always puts the best bait on the hook.

John T. Malloy in *Dress for Success* explains the effect of grooming on success. There are two ideas in this book that I would like to emphasize. One is that, while good grooming and proper dress may not make up for other inadequacies, improper and radical dress and grooming definitely will stand in the way of success. This is true because most of us succeed or fail through the help or hindrance that comes to us from those who already are in a position to help or hinder. This is a reality that cannot be ignored.

The other idea in Malloy's book that I wish to emphasize is that grooming and dress have an effect on discipline, work habits, and attitudes. It seems that a person is making a statement about himself or herself when he or she dresses and grooms. And this statement affects conduct in ways that have a bearing on success and failure. Also, dress and grooming affect interpretation of conduct. A quiet and withdrawn deportment may be called surly if the person is unkempt, whereas it may be called humility if the person is well groomed. Again, an unkempt person may be saying, "I hate myself"; but his appearance may be interpreted as a declaration of hate for the manager of the firm in which he is seeking a position. Still further, a sloppy person may be saying, "I am so satisfied with myself that I do not need any of the props that insecure people use." But the officer behind the desk who is scrutinizing him may be thinking, "This person lacks the discipline and organization for the demanding position he is seeking." (New York: Warner Books.)

Of course, the above is not an exact quote from Malloy; but it is my expansion on the ideas I gleaned from his book. One may not wish to fully subscribe to everything Malloy says; but the priesthood and ladies of promise would profit from reading his book.

A second commitment, closely related to good grooming, is the commitment to keep your apartments or homes clean, even before you are married and especially after you are married. There is something orderly about being orderly. When your mind is orderly, people see that. Orderliness is one of the things about my wife that has impressed me. Within three or four minutes after we get up in the morning our bed is made. She has rarely left the bedroom without making the bed first. In spite of having seven children and their friends and the other things that go with it, I haven't been embarrassed to have company come to our home. I haven't had to run around and grab all sorts of things from the living room floor and get them out of sight. She really is just terrific. And this is a common trait in wives of men who are called to responsibility in the Church and in business. They generally are neat and orderly and have learned to keep their houses clean. Of course, there are other strong qualities that give women charm and grace. But I think orderliness is a very critical commitment. Sisters, if a man is going to be able to support you and become what you can be proud of, you certainly can have a lot to do with it by sending him forth and welcoming him back in neatness and cleanliness in the haven where he gets his strength, regeneration, and motivation.

We are in a time when the home and the traditional role of women are under attack. Perhaps some of the traditional ideas do need reexamination. But the more I learn about who opposes these traditional ideas, the more I am willing to let the inspired prophets of God give us direction and leadership as we move cautiously forward in these troubled times. Perhaps there are homes in which the husband can rightly help provide some of the internal orderliness by helping with the housework. That is an internal matter that needs to be negotiated behind closed doors by those involved. But whatever you work out, try always to be aware of the divine and eternal ideal and work ever in that direction. That is the route to the greatest joy; but it is a path of peace, not strife.

Orderliness promotes peace of mind and efficiency. If beds are made when people get up, if clothes are put away when taken off, if dishes are returned to shelves after use, a load is lifted from the mind that otherwise bears down and robs a part of the mental and emotional energy that is needed to get through the day. In our home we are apt to have our dishes gathered and washed before we are through with them. But if your wife isn't that way, brethren, remember that nagging wastes far more time than pitching in and helping get the job done, or, at least, started. Besides, it will help create habits that will be useful at work.

A third commitment that deserves a lot of attention is physical conditioning. Good conditioning improves appearance, enhances grooming, and prepares for those emergencies when extra demands are placed on us. This is a relative commitment because of the differences in physical capabilities. For instance, there are many who have been injured or who have inherent weaknesses. Everything has to be taken into account. Still it is a truism that most of us can improve our physical conditioning, and the improvement will show in appearances and in production. Some of the most inspiring examples of physical fitness have come to us from men and women in wheelchairs.

I think there does come a time occasionally when most of us need to stretch physically to see how much we can take. Emergencies arise and we are forced into something very strenuous. These are the times when heart attacks occur if we haven't prepared ourselves in advance. It is wise to build up fitness gradually if possible. Then, when the demand comes, we are in the physical condition to handle it more safely. If you have ever been in really great physical condition sometime in your life, you may realize that somewhere between that and where you most likely are there is a good standard that is compatible with your normal activity.

This principle was impressed on my mind when I was on a high council. I went to a distant city on business with a fine member of the Church. We had to make a connection in San Francisco. It was about a half a mile from the arrival concourse back in and down to the other end of the terminal. We both had our suitcases and started to run with them in hand as we only had so many minutes to make the connection. I got to the plane first and said, "Hold up; I have a friend coming. He will be here in about the next thirty seconds." When I saw my friend, I was frightened. I thought he was going to have a heart attack and die before he even got on the plane. His countenance was gray and he almost collapsed into his seat. I was still puffing and panting myself as we sat there recovering. I realized that we had had a close call that would have been just an exhilarating experience if we had been practicing some principles of constant physical conditioning.

It would be good to be able, when or if the time comes, to equal the performance of a father in his fifties or sixties who climbed up Mount Olympus with us several years back to search for his son who was presumed lost up there. A lot of us went up for hours at a stretch, but the father was on Mount Olympus for three days and three nights without leaving the mountain. As a young man I was in a lot better condition than the father, but my motivation was different. I had gone on a search party to find someone; but he had gone to look for his son; and he would not come down off the mountain. He stayed there and walked, and you know how tired you can get climbing mountains. It was June or July and plenty hot. But the impressive thing is that he didn't have a heart attack—and he was able to go through that ordeal. I think we need occasionally to be able to do something like that and be in good enough condition to survive. Life has a way of putting physical demands on us and we just need to be able to meet these demands.

The other side of this coin is wisdom. If we get into a demanding situation, we need to have the wisdom not to exceed our capacities. This even can be a day-by-day challenge. Getting adequate daily rest is an important part of proper conditioning. I used to tell my missionaries, "I really don't care if you take a nap when you come in at lunch. In fact, I really would like you to because ten to fifteen minutes on the floor will make your study much more effective and you won't be dropping your head and going to sleep with your mind wandering." I think one reason the prophet has been able to survive and accomplish so much is the fact that he can take a nap on the floor somewhere in his office during the day. Those who cannot take short naps and gain some needed rest must learn to plan to get adequate rest. They may be the high-strung type who can get into serious health problems if they do not learn to relax and rest properly.

A fourth principle of preparation to walk in high places is a positive mental attitude. I think it was Paul H. Dunn who said that he was speaking before a group of businessmen who looked like they had been weaned on lemon juice through a dill pickle. That is pretty descriptive of a few groups to whom I have had to speak. A speaker in that situation needs a positive attitude.

Probably you all know about the Dale Carnegie memory course. Elder Marion D. Hanks once said, "You know, they have this remembering names program by, who is it? Tom Carnegin or somebody."

In that program they expect you to wake up in the morning with a positive attitude. If you wake up and think, *Oh, man, there's the alarm!* that is negative. You have to go back and start over again. You set the alarm for five minutes later and the alarm goes off and you think, *Oh, man! It's time to get up!* Really positive, you see.

In the mission field you jump out of bed at 6:30 A.M. and run to the shower and your companion has used all the hot water; but you say, "Boy, I love cold showers at 6:30 in the morning." You go to breakfast, and your companion has made hotcakes that are raw in the middle; but you say, "I love raw-in-the-middle pancakes." Because there are a lot of problems that can cause us to become very negative and ominous and, I suppose, dwarf what we really are trying to do, I think a positive outlook is important. A positive attitude is a part of the personalities of those who achieve.

Learning to love work is a fifth commitment that will prepare us to walk in high places. Remember Elder Thomas S. Monson's *W* formula: "Work will win when wishy-washy wishing won't." I believe that if there is one common quality among achievers, it is that they love work more than nonachievers do. I think it is important for us sometimes to push ourselves beyond our usual limits so that we can learn our true capacities for work. I think we need to be in the kind of physical condition and mental attitude to do this.

Among other sacrifices, a person who walks in high places may have to get by with less sleep occasionally just to know he can do it when the need is really there. As I have mentioned earlier, my mother often had to forego the usual amount and time of sleep when I was young. One of the highest places I have ever walked was in her shadow. I saw an older brother who grew up fast and was able to go to work at fourteen in the Bauer Mines near Tooele because he was large of stature. He became the example to all of us who were his younger brothers and sisters. These family examples taught me how to work. And when I did get a job, I knew the family was depending on me to hold it.

I had worked for a five-store grocery chain all the way through junior high and high school. I continued with them full time upon graduating from high school, a total of eight years altogether. Then, when Albertson's came to Salt Lake, I thought maybe my chances of moving up would increase because it wasn't just a local firm. So I made an appointment with the district manager and went home and discussed it with my wife. That night I went over and over it in my mind. In fact, I am convinced that I did not sleep. Everything hinged on getting this new job; and I felt that I didn't have the confidence I needed to sell myself to Albertson's supervisor. I wanted very much to go to work for this different company. As I prepared through the night, I went over the interview a thousand times it seemed. Every time I thought of a question the district manager might ask, I would ask myself again, *Why do you want to go to work for Albertson's?* I responded in my mind to that question I can't tell you how many different times or in how many different ways.

The next day I went to see the man and had to wait for him quite a while after the time of the appointment. I waited. I was dressed the best I possibly could in my only suit, a gray one.

I commend that to you when you go to look for a job. Don't go in your grubbies. Go as if you are in earnest about looking for a job. When you need a job, don't just go thinking, *Here's an ad in the paper, I'll respond to that and go home again.* Work at looking for a job. Go looking eight hours a day if you don't have one. You have nothing better to do, and that's the most important thing you need to do—get a job and get lined up and then work the way you ought to work. So, I'd suggest again, when you go looking for a job, work at it like it is your job. Work at it eight hours or ten or twelve hours a day until you get it.

Finally the Albertson's district manager came out to interview me. We interviewed back and forth for about twenty minutes. Then he said, "Well, the best we can offer you is $68 for a forty-hour week." This was 1954. I was making $107 at the time. We talked a little longer and he said that he thought they could go to $78 for a forty-hour week. I just couldn't make it on that. My car had broken down. We barely had enough money for house payments. How was I going to go to work and make ends meet and take care of tithing and other Church assessments and obligations? I remember telling the district manager that I really needed the job. I wanted opportunity. I promised him that if they would hire me I would do the best it was humanly possible for me to do or they could fire me and not pay me a penny. I could not have been more sincere.

"I'll tell you what we'll do," he said. "We'll give you $78 plus eight hours overtime which will be about $104 per week. That's the most we can give. We're only paying our department heads $110. Now, you go home and decide if you want to go to work for us, and we'll decide overnight whether we want to hire you."

Although a cut of twelve dollars a month wasn't much, it was a lot on our scanty means. I told my wife what the salary would be and said, "I'm going to go. Will you support me?" Of course, she said she would.

The next morning I went down to my old job as I normally did; and at 9:00 A.M. as the store opened in walked five of the executives from Albertson's. They walked down through the produce department which I co-managed, examined it, said hello to me, left, and called me back in a little while and said they'd like to hire me. So I asked how soon. This was about May. "We'll hire you October fourth." I had to keep that a secret all that time, and I had to maintain the enthusiasm on the job that I had had before. It was one of the real tests of my life.

When I went to work for Albertson's, I just simply put my heart and soul into it and fifteen months later they made me the supervisor of an entire district. I believe in a success formula I picked up somewhere. The essence of this formula is that promotions come more rapidly to those who work harder and longer hours. The harder and longer you work, the sooner the promotions come. Of course, a Latter-day Saint will want to remember the family and other Church commitments so that his or her success will not destroy the very reasons for succeeding.

I believe that the work ethic is an attitude. It is a discipline. It is something that can become a habit. By that I mean that when you work fast and hard or when you are intense in studying, it becomes a habit; and every time you study, you study with that habit. When you read, you read in that habitual way. When you work, you work fast and hard if that is a habit. If you have developed the habit of sloth and laziness then those things stay with you; and every time you work, you work at that same slow pace and you don't get anything done. There is an excitement when the blood starts coursing through the veins and you are working fast. You think faster. You think more clearly. I believe there is a purging that takes place. President Harold B. Lee said, "The greatest poverty is the poverty of desire." I really believe that. When someone said that you are the light on the hill either for good or evil, he really meant it, To the Church, the leaders are the light. I believe that no other Church has the discipline and the government and the order that we do; and I am speaking now of work. Our people really are traditionally trained to work.

Warm human relations—how you get along with other people—is a sixth commitment I would like to recommend. It is closely related to work. Work and drive have a lot to do with human relations. We get along with others best when we feel the best about ourselves. And hard work is one of the greatest solutions to a poor self-image. In fact, I think learning to work hard and getting a strong testimony will cure almost all self-image problems.

If you are going to be uncommon and realize your potential, you must have this human-relations factor in correct operation. We really have to be warm, friendly, and kind. I realize that I am not going to please everyone, and I have to carry that on my heart. But I am not going to suffer over it and become negative. I still have to be pleased with myself and live with myself when I get through with whatever I have to do. So I want to be kind and warm. And when someone comes up after a meeting and says, "That was really a lousy speech," I'll just have to salvage my ego by saying to myself, *That is his opinion. I really did the best I could with my limited talents.* I have to live with myself on things like that.

I have watched the people that I admire most, that I love most, respect most, and want most to be like, and I haven't met any of them who don't have outstanding abilities in a human-relations way. Wherever they are, you see them visiting people with kindness and understanding. They know how to listen and really be interested. They understand the things that affect and help human relations.

Maybe the hardest preparation for walking in high places is this seventh one that I now would like to get you to think about. It is the task of learning to think. Elder Thomas S. Monson said, "Thinking. Thinking is the hardest work we go through." Dr. Hugh Nibley said something like this: "The mind will take a terrible revenge if one does not think on constructive things. It will reach out and grasp anything that is nearby. It is being worked all of the time, twenty-four hours a day. Consciously or subconsciously, it is involved." So, controlled thinking is the hardest work we do and it is the very essence of life, the meaning of being.

Thinking is mostly talking to yourself. The better vocabulary you have, the better this thinking can become. That is, it can get into things that are uncommon and things that test your mental strength. When we talk about controlled thinking, we are talking about this business of stretching our thinking capacity by vocabulary improvement. We also—and maybe more importantly—are talking about saying no to Satan when he attempts to invade and take over our minds. We must learn to turn that channel off if we wish to stay in control. That is the very basic meaning of intelligence as it is defined in the Doctrine and Covenants: "The glory of God is intelligence, or, in other words, light and truth. Light and truth forsake that evil one." (D&C 93:36-37.) Where do we forsake the "evil one"? In the dark recesses of our minds. That is where he lurks and attempts to take control. So flood the light on him and cast him out so that you can maintain control. Now, I am not saying that Satan himself is actually lurking in the dark recesses of your mind. Let me explain it with an analogy. Suppose you were a television set and you were being used to view pornography on some cable service. Then the television set would be invaded by evil. If you pick up negative, evil, or useless thoughts, you are allowing the spirit of the evil one to communicate to you and take control. Weak and ignoble thinking becomes a habit, and bad habits are the chains that are described in Alma 12:9-11. They take away light and truth.

Another important part of the thinking commitment is mental ambition. We would not have a good balance in this life if all of our work were simply physical. I think going out and working on a farm or in the yard until the perspiration just pours off is a great purging experience. The mind needs to go through that same kind of purging. We need to think so seriously sometimes that our heads almost ache when we finish. We have all been involved in that kind of intensity at some time. When it is over there is a refreshment that comes and a feeling of accomplishment and peace because of the exertion.

This mental wrestling can take the form of prolonged prayer. It may be necessary to pray longer and harder sometimes in order to get the feeling that you have been heard. You remember the case of Enos and his day-long prayer. Of course, that was an extreme case involving a future prophet of God. If you ever get where you need to pray all day long, you will know it and the power will be given to you. It isn't the sort of thing you just set out to do because you would like to hear a voice like Enos did. Still, Enos's example is one you should ponder as you think of gaining the determination to think and communicate with God. There are lessons for everybody in the story of Enos.

We have discussed seven principles or commitments that help us prepare to walk in high places. There are others, of course. Let me now ask a few questions about your ambitions, your objectives, and your goals. These are questions you should ask yourselves often.

First, what do you really want out of life? Emerson said that if you will pay the price, you can have it.

If you could choose one person to be like, who would it be? Think about that. Who you choose tells you a lot about yourself.

What are you willing to do to reach your goals? Some experts who study things like this have said that if you take one hudnred men when they are twenty-five and start them all out at the same time with the same goal, that only five of them will reach the goal by the time they retire. The goal will have faded out of the sight of the other ninety-five. Are you a fader, or do you stick to your commitments once they have been wisely made?

When are you going to start? A very critical question. Remember that Jacob said that the way is narrow, but the path is directly in front of your feet. (2 Nephi 9:41.) It is always there.

Where will you find the opportunities? Edward R. Sill wrote a verse entitled "Opportunity" that I memorized. It was about a prince and a coward. The coward broke his sword as an excuse to flee the battlefield. Later the prince, wounded and weaponless, came across the coward's sword and used it to turn the tide of battle and win a victory. Will you recognize your opportunities?

What do you want to achieve in the particular field of your choice, be it religion or politics or whatever? Only specific goals are useful.

You will find part of the answer to all of the above questions in the preparations you make for success.

Giordano Bruno, an Italian philosopher, made a great discovery as a young man while running through the beautiful, flower-covered hills near his home in Italy. He discovered that no matter where he ran, or how far, he always remained the center of the universe. This is impressive to me; because each one of us is in the center of the universe. I thought about this as I visited in New York some time ago. While there, everything was revolving around me. Of course, I thought about home and had concerns that my family would be protected while I was away; but my world was a different world. You have all had this experience. The gospel of Jesus Christ teaches us to reach out beyond the center of the universe and therein we will find the great joy of life. We visualize Heavenly Father and his Great Son in the center of the universe, and we see ourselves one day in the center of our own universe — a vastly greater one than the one which revolves about us here. Then we think about how our Heavenly Father became what he is. Then we see that service and love are a great part of it. And that begins to shape our goals and attitudes. And we see that life calls for preparation and commitments.

3

The Realm of the Final Inch: Planning With Commitment

There's a story about a farmer who fails to get his work done because he lacks firm commitment. Though I have changed the details, it goes something like this. The farmer told his wife he was going out to mow the north forty. On his way to the machine shed, he noticed a loose board on the corn crib. So he went to look for a hammer and some nails which he remembered leaving on the back porch. This led him through the garden which he noticed was quite weedy. He decided to weed a row of carrots, telling himself that he ought to weed a row a day. About two-thirds of the way down the carrot row he straightened up to rest his back and, looking over his shoulder, he saw he had left the gate open and some hens had come into the garden and were scratching up his sweet corn. It took about fifteen minutes to get them out and back into the hen yard. It took another half hour to mend the hole through which they were getting out. After that he figured he had just as well gather the eggs. As he began to do so, he noticed that the nests needed more straw; so he left the eggs and went after a bale of straw. As he was about to pick up the straw, he noticed his pitchfork had a broken handle and remembered that he hadn't fixed it. So he went to the machine shop to hunt for the new handle he had bought. While hunting, he stumbled across the mowing machine and remembered he was going to spend the day mowing. It wasn't much past 10:00 A.M.; so he decided to return to his original plan. Only he remembered he hadn't greased the mower. He started to hunt for his grease gun. After some searching he remembered that he had left it in the garage. When he found it, it was empty, and he didn't have a refill. So he got in his car and went to town to get some grease. As he passed Sleepy Corners he stopped at Sleepy Joe's for a doughnut and a glass of milk. Some of the boys were there, and he learned that the bass were biting down at the reservoir south of town. He got home about lunch time. After lunch, on his way to the machine shed he stumbled over the hoe he had left in the garden. He remembered hoeing up some worms and decided to see if he could find some to set aside for some evening fishing. It didn't take long to get a can of worms. At this point he decided the day was pretty well shot anyway, and he had just as well go fishing right now instead of waiting until evening.

The opposite of this sort of aimlessness is well-directed persistence based on proper planning. Persistence eventually and finally wins. Sometimes worthwhile things come easily; but usually they come hard and slow.

In *The First Circle* Aleksandr Solzhenitsyn tells about the realm of the final inch. It is a beautiful concept.

> "How to face difficulties?" he declared again. "In the realm of the unknown, difficulties must be viewed as a *hidden treasure!* Usually, the more difficult, the better. It's not as valuable if your difficulties stem from your own inner struggle. But when difficulties arise out of increasing objective resistance, that's *marvelous!*" . . .
> "The most rewarding path of investigation is: 'the greatest external resistance in the presence of the least internal resistance.' Failures must be considered the cue for further application of effort and concentration of will power. And if substantial efforts have already been made, the failures are all the more joyous. It means that our crowbar has struck the iron box containing the treasure. Overcoming the increased difficulties is all the more valuable be-

cause in failure the *growth of the person performing the task* takes place in proportion to the difficulty encountered! . . .

"And now listen: The rule of the Final Inch! The realm of the Final Inch! In the Language of Maximum Clarity it is immediately clear what that is. The work has been almost completed, the goal almost attained, everything seems completely right and the difficulties overcome. But the quality of the thing is not *quite* right. Finishing touches are needed, maybe still more research. In that moment of fatigue and self-satisfaction it is especially tempting to leave the work without having attained the apex of quality. Work in the area of the Final Inch is very, very complex and also especially valuable, because it is executed by the most perfected means. In fact, the rule of the Final Inch consists in this: not to shirk this crucial work. Not to postpone it, for the thoughts of the person performing the task will then stray from the realm of the Final Inch. And not to mind the time spent on it, knowing that one's purpose lies not in completing things faster but in the attainment of perfection." (Thomas P. Whitney, trans. [New York: Harper and Row, 1968], page 139.)

He says that this final-inch concept works better on external problems in our lives than it does on internal problems. You have an internal problem—one inside of you—when you are jealous or worried about someone else or don't have any drive. In this case the realm of the final inch is not as clearly applicable. Internal problems are harder to solve than external problems. But if the problem is external (like most of the problems we wrestle with in making a living and working in the Church), the concept of the realm of the final inch is really valuable. It is like digging down into a hole and coming to the treasure. When you hit the problem, it is like hitting your shovel on a buried treasure. Because there is where the growth comes. Solzhenitsyn says that most of us get the project just about finished and we are satisfied and let it drop there. But if we are aware of the importance of the realm of the final inch, we make that extra effort and take that extra time to go that extra bit and put in that extra elbow grease to give the task the polish that will make us really happy to present it to whomever requested it, whether it be staff work in an organization or a contract out in the market place. Then when the questions come up from priesthood leaders, employers, customers, or department leaders, we have the answers because we have worked hard and fully in the realm of the final inch. The final inch can take as much time and effort as all the rest. Probably the majority do not give it any time. But the finishers, the fully committed, do — and they are the happy souls who are responsible for most worthwhile achievements. In addition to other successes, they usually get the best jobs and are the least likely to lose their jobs. Of course, we mustn't make the mistake of assuming there will be no setbacks in this life and that everything will always be fair. But it is very shortsighted to let that keep us from becoming a finisher.

Even people of commitment sometimes overlook the importance of that careful preparation that comes from the kind of planning that uses a lot of foresight. I remember an embarrassing episode out of my own life that shows the value of planning in the realm of the final inch wherein potential disasters are foreseen and forestalled.

I served on the missionary committee when I was a young man still in my thirties. One of our assignments was to travel with the General Authorities and talk about missionary work. This led to other requests to speak. One time in 1967, a fellow committee member, T. Bowring Woodbury, had a speaking assignment that he couldn't fulfill. He called and said, "Vaughn, I have a speaking assignment in Orem." (That's a town just northwest of where Brigham Young University is situated.) "I'd like you to go in my place and talk about missionary work." He gave me the date and I told him I'd be delighted to go.

About a week before I was to go he called up and said, "Now, you haven't forgotten to go down to Orem next week have you?" I said I hadn't.

"You're sure nothing has come up?"

"No, Brother Woodbury, it hasn't. I'll be there."

"All right. I'm just double checking."

Then the day before I was to go, he called me again and said, "How is your car?" You can see that President Woodbury was a man of the final inch.

I said, "Well, we have two. My wife has one and I have one. Why?"

"I just want to know if you want to borrow my Cadillac. It has snow tires in case it snows or something."

"No, don't worry, Brother Woodbury. I've got a car and I'll get down there."

The next day he called up again about 2:00 P.M. and said, "Did you see what is outside?"

I replied, "Yes, it has been snowing all day."

"Are your snow tires good enough to get you down to Orem?" he asked.

I said, "Yes, sir, they are."

"You're sure you don't want to trade cars with me?"

"Don't worry," I answered. "I have snow treads and I can make it."

Brother Woodbury was a great planner. In fact, you might even say that he was an inspired planner in this case.

My wife called just after he did and said she had to go to the doctor and asked if I minded if she came down and dropped her car off and took mine. She said her appointment was at 2:30 and she would easily be home in plenty of time. "What time were you planning on leaving?"

I said, "I am speaking at 8:00 P.M.. I had better leave at 6:00 P.M. because it is snowing and I don't want to have any problems."

I went home at 5:00 P.M. in my wife's car, and my car wasn't there. Neither was my wife. I went into the house and thought I had better get cleaned up because she would be there soon. I got all ready and it was six o'clock. My talk was prepared, and she still hadn't come. I thought, *Well, I had better wait. I don't want to take her car. I don't know if there are any problems with it, and I do know what my car will do.*

So I waited around and pretty soon it was 6:15 and I

thought, *It's only 35 or 40 miles down to Orem. That's no problem. Her car will go that far at least or she shouldn't be driving it anyway.*

So I went out and got in her car after leaving her a note that said, "Some doctor's appointment—from 2:30 until whatever time you finally get home!" There was just a little bit of sarcasm in my note, I admit.

Anyway, I took off and started down Ninth East out toward the Draper turn-off. All of a sudden the temperature gauge was all the way over on and beyond boiling. I thought, *What is this? Boy, I'm glad I left early.*

I pulled into a gas station and said to the man who met me, "There is something wrong with my car. Would you mind checking it out?" He lifted the hood and looked around. I tell you, I met in that gas station the slowest human being in the world. He fiddled around with my car. He worked with it, and finally said, "One of your fan belts is broken."

I said, "Great. Would you mind putting one on for me?"

It was the third one in. He took off the first one and then he took off the second one, and here I was marching back and forth. I think he started getting a little excited as he could see me. Finally he reached up on the wall and said, "You know, I haven't the right size. I'll tell you what I'll do. We've got a station down on State Street, and I'll send one of my men down to get the right-sized one."

So he yelled to another man in the coffee shop across the street, and I met the second slowest man in the world. He moseyed across the street and climbed into his car and took off. By this time it was 6:30 and then 6:40 and then 6:45 and the guy still hadn't come back. When he had been gone about twenty minutes I said, "Just put my car back together. I'd rather try it like this or go somewhere else."

So he started getting a little excited. He put the two fan belts on. About that time this fellow came squealing into the gas station trying to impress us. He had the fan belt and I said, "Take them back off. I'd better stay and have the fan belt put on."

So he took off the outer two and tried this one on, and it

was the wrong size. By this time it was ten till seven. I told them to put my car back together. I drove out to our Sandy store and said to the assistant manager, "Harley, I've got an appointment down in Orem. I wonder if I could leave my car here and borrow yours. I'll be back by 9:30 or 10:00. I'll leave my car here in case you need it. It doesn't have a fan belt, but at least you could drive a little way without any problems."

He said, "Golly, you could borrow it; but it is an open jeep and there is a lot of snow on the seat."

I said, "Well, maybe I'd better take my own car."

I thought, *This is for the Lord, and I don't know much about cars.* So I just jumped in. *We'll do it,* I thought. I forgot how many times I had learned that the Lord helps only after we have done all we can do. Even then there has to be a very good reason that involves the Lord's plans as well as ours. I am not saying that prayers are not helpful or won't be answered. But the purpose of this life would be frustrated if we had it as easy as we sometimes want it.

I headed out, and the water gauge went over to boiling. Then all of a sudden the temperature started dropping a little bit and I thought, *Isn't it great what prayer will do?* I don't know why, but it started dropping down until it was just about boiling. Then as I started up over the Point of the Mountain, all of a sudden it went all the way back and hung over to the right as far as it would go, and the motor started crackling and sparking. I'm not joking. I unlocked the door and cracked it open so that if the car exploded I could dive out into the snow. It was getting that hot.

I got past the Point of the Mountain and was coming down the other side and I saw Jay Lambert's gas station and thought, *What a break! I'll pull in.* So I did, but everything was closed.

It was about 7:30 by then, and I still had half an hour; so I decided to go out and hitchhike, as my car wouldn't start. There was a telephone booth there; I called up the family of the man who had invited Brother Woodbury to speak and said, "This is Vaughn Featherstone. My car has broken down out around the

Point of the Mountain at Jay Lambert's gas station. I'm about a half an hour out of Orem, but I'll go out and hitchhike; and if I can get a ride, I'll be there even if it is a little late." I hung up, and she called her husband at the ward house and gave him the message.

I went out and started hitchhiking. It isn't easy to get a ride when it is really snowing. I was in my black suit with a black top coat over it. I must have looked like the devil standing out there. They would see me and just go shooting right on past. Finally at about 8:15 I hadn't got a ride and I thought, *Even if I get a ride now, it will be 8:45 before I get to Orem; and by the time I get to the ward house, it will be about time for the closing prayer.*

After a few more minutes I walked across the street and thought I'd go back to Salt Lake. I was just feeling terrible. As luck would have it, the first car passed me, slowed down, turned around, and came back. The driver was a professor from BYU who, I guess, wasn't afraid of the devil. He stopped and picked me up and took me right to my door. I walked in about 9:15, and my wife wasn't there. That was a blessing. I went into my den and sat down with all the lights off. The thing that kept going over in my mind was T. Bowring Woodbury. He had foreseen all the problems and had done everything he could to get me there; and I had turned down all his offers of help. Now, I would have to call him the next day and say that I didn't make it. What made matters worse was that this particular stake had had only four convert baptisms during the whole year and they averaged only about six hours of proselyting per stake missionary. I was going down there with the theme "No matter how valid, an excuse never changes performance." Well, I really learned a great lesson about final-inch preparation.

Probably most of the people who have stumbled over a gold nugget have gone to their graves thinking they stumbled over a rock. You at least have to know what a gold nugget looks like so that if you stumble over one you can recognize what it is when you look back at it. As is usually the case in a disastrous experience, there was a gold nugget in my experience with T.

Bowring Woodbury's speaking assignment. It was the rocky fact that we aren't able to meet commitments until we are prepared to cope with all reasonable contingencies. There were at least three things I could have done, any one of which would have forestalled the disaster: 1) saw to it that my wife's car was in good shape, 2) traded cars with Brother Woodbury when I traded cars with my wife, or, 3) thereafter called Brother Woodbury and borrowed his Cadillac as soon as I suspected possible trouble.

I am happy to be able to say that failing to meet commitments has never been a habit with me. But I occasionally get caught in the backwash of human error. I do not excuse myself. We should try to foresee and forestall all possible operations of the so-called Murphy's Law. That's the law that says, in one version of many, "Nature is on the side of the hidden flaw." I know that we can find no end of examples to prove that; but I believe that the Lord is on the side of any and all who prepare as best they can and then go ahead prayerfully. The better we plan, the less likely we are to get caught by a hidden flaw and the more worthy we will be of the Lord's intervention in our behalf.

The idea is to have all bases covered, like the boy who went home with the worst report card ever. He presented it to his father even though he hated to do so. His father looked at it, and it was just deplorable. He commented that he had never seen a more terrible report card than this one, and the son said, "Yes, dad, what do you think the problem is? Heredity or environment?" The boy thought that covered his tracks pretty well; but he found that it didn't.

As long as we are on the subject of schools and students, I think it is proper to state that a lot of cheating on exams is due to lack of foresight. The student doesn't foresee the pressure he is going to be under when he has the exam right in front of him and realizes that he isn't prepared. Then temptation becomes too great. A few years ago I had a colleague on the Missionary Committee who commented that one reason he never had cheated as a student was that he had more confidence in his own knowledge than in that of anyone he sat by. He said, "I've noticed that most cheaters don't have good judgment about where to look for the right answers."

I can illustrate this with another story. This one is about a student who apparently had been cheating. The teacher called the father in, and the father said, "I don't believe my son, Adam, would cheat."

The teacher said, "We have proof."

"What is your proof?"

"The first question was Who was the sixteenth president of the United States? The fellow across the aisle from your son wrote Abraham Lincoln and your son, Adam, wrote Abraham Lincoln.

The father said, "Well, they could both be right."

"Yes, but the second question was the tip-off: Who was the seventeenth president of the United States? The fellow across the aisle wrote Lyndon B. Johnson and your son wrote Lyndon B. Johnson."

The father said, "Well, they could both be wrong."

The teacher said, "Well, the third question was the clincher: What were the causes of the Civil War? The fellow across the aisle wrote I don't know, and your son wrote Neither do I."

A religion teacher at BYU told about a student who wanted to be a medical doctor; so he enrolled in a pre-med program. This course brought him face to face with some classes that proved very hard. He wondered if this wasn't a sign that God didn't want him to be a doctor. It seemed reasonable to him that God would make it easy for him to become what God wanted him to become. His religion teacher used the story of Nephi getting the Brass Plates as a means of showing this young man that the Lord doesn't remove the obstacles from the paths we are to follow—whether we choose those paths or God chooses them. Usually the only time we should give up a path is when we learn that it was chosen unwisely and is leading us into something that will take us off the path that leads to the celestial kingdom. When we know we have planned well, we must have the commitment to push the plan through to success.

I can illustrate this with a story about a young man from a little town in Idaho who became chief executive officer of a corporation that was doing seven billion dollars in sales every year. A few years ago I had the privilege of visiting him for about four hours in his New York office. The year before, this company, a large grocery chain, lost 157 million dollars. That would be the annual income of all the wage earners of between fifty and a hundred typical American LDS wards, depending on where you picked them. Of course, that would not be counting the welfare cases or the very wealthy. Put another way, 157 million would pay a salary of twenty thousand dollars to 7,850 families for a year.

Contrary to what many people believe, big grocery corporations rarely have a final net profit of more than 1 or 2 percent and cannot survive large losses. This particular corporation faced closing its doors and putting many thousands of people out of work. Again, contrary to popular belief, big corporations consider it a sacred obligation to maintain high employment. It is built into the dynamics of the way big business operates just as it is built into the dynamics of the way big government operates. Only big business cannot tax; therefore, it has to make a profit or go into receivership.

This young man from Idaho was hired as chief executive to cure the problem. He knew the cure was going to hurt; because he had to close stores that couldn't be brought back to profitability in order to save the stores that were making a profit or could be brought up to profitability. He was hired in February. By October the company had closed 1,321 stores. Their sales for the following year were equal to what they had been before the 1,321 stores were closed. To get this change effected, they had to change many top executives. This chief executive told me, "When I went to work for that company, I studied the executive situation and realized that I would have to change 75 percent of these high-paid men to save the jobs of the thousands who were facing unemployment because of loose and faulty supervision. This would not be an easy task. Other men have had this same plan and made that same commitment to themselves before they went to work for a new organization. I made it; and then after I became acquainted with the executives I knew I must change, I started thinking about these men. I thought, *This is a great man. We couldn't find anyone better on the outside.* But I knew that was wrong. These executives had to be moved out to break up a failure-acceptance pattern. I'd go home and look in the mirror and say, 'You must, you must keep the commitment. You've got to keep that commitment.' I kept the commitment; but every single night I'd have to go home and tell myself the same thing: 'You've got to keep the commitment you made because it was right when you were thinking clearly. Now don't let anything cloud your thinking.' "

Now you can see a turnabout in this company almost like electricity. You can feel the vibrations when you walk into the corporate headquarters. It isn't sleeping anymore. It is a giant. I think this experience of a successful executive teaches us the lesson that we must be willing to do the hard things. Sooner or later we all come face to face with them. If our commitment is strong, we will be able to do the hard things that lead to success whether it is saving fifty thousand corporate jobs or getting through a tough college course enroute to a demanding profession.

Some people—maybe most now days—think the 1,321 stores shouldn't have been closed and the executives replaced. All they can see is the temporary unemployment caused by the shake-up. They cannot see the greater unemployment and displacement that would have occurred if the whole corporation had failed and gone under. And they cannot see the great economic loss in the inefficiency of the old and failing leadership of a corporation that is floundering in the seas of complacency, red tape, and regulation, and about to sink to the bottom. And they cannot see the growth and new jobs created since the ship was rescued.

There is one principle that we must remember as we go along trying to do things right and be successful. You might call it the principle of carry-over. That is, when you overcome one fault, it becomes easier to overcome another. This may explain why chastity is so important to success. I mean real success, of course. A person may be very successful in his chosen field of economic endeavor and still have his life in a shambles. Nothing is so devastating to a life as unchastity. I don't know of a truly great man who is immoral. I am saying who *is* immoral. Those who have been immoral can overcome the problem. It can be erased and forgotten through repentance. Even among non-members and non-Christians the act of reformation, the discarding of evil practices, has a profound effect on the whole life of the person who reforms. Of course, he cannot become a celestial being without the application of the principles of the gospel. His reformation, without faith in Christ, baptism, the laying on of hands, etc., is not full repentance; but it is a great step toward full repentance. And it will have a profound effect on other aspects of that person's life. There will be a carry-over to other principles of success. It will be easier to be persistent, to work hard on the final inch.

Let me share an idea that came from Emerson. He said we can have anything we want. All we have to do is pay the price and take it. That works in both directions. Anyone reading this, if he or she wants to, can be immoral. It is just that simple. But you have to pay the price; and I want to tell you that the price would stagger you if you knew what it is. If you ever pay the price yourself or have occasion to help someone else through the sorrow of paying the price, you will learn what a dear price you pay for immorality. Sometimes people turn it around and think they are giving up a lot to be chaste—a lot of what? Peace of mind? Happy families? Eternal joy? Self-respect? The respect and confidence of others? Freedom from divorce and other legal entanglements? It isn't a sacrifice to pass up sin and its aftermath.

One man who came to me for help to get back into fellowship told me that he had been married in the temple. He knew what would happen if he was unfaithful to his wife. He knew what it would do to his children. He thought of excommunication, his family's embarrassment, possible separation and divorce and still chose a route to disaster for a few moments of what he supposed would be great pleasure. As he sat before me, he said he didn't know what came over him; but there he was. He had risked everything he held dear, and it had proved to be a small plan.

President Kimball once said, "Make no small plans. They have no magic to stir men's souls." I was very impressed when he said that. His life has been a living example of that. Think about President Kimball and what has been done in his relatively short ministry. We have expanded from about seventeen thousand missionaries to nearly double that. We have added many new missions. The work is going across the earth as it never has before. Temples have been announced all over the world. President Kimball made no small plans. And you would have to look long and hard to find a person who was more committed to the great plans he planned.

4

The Inspiration of Great Books

Some time ago I served as a mission president in the Texas San Antonio Mission. One day in Harlingen a good brother handed me a large, thick volume and said, "I would like you to read this book." The book was *Happy Homes and the Hearts That Make Them*, by Samuel Smiles.

I said, "Thanks, but I have enough reading to last through my mission."

He pushed the book into my hands and said, "I want you to read it. Don't worry about bringing it back until you finish it."

I said as kindly as I could, "Thanks, but I really don't have time for it."

He would not take no for an answer. Finally I took the book and told him I would return it when I was back in Harlingen in two weeks.

I carried the volume home with me on the plane. I took it to the office and placed it on my desk where it would be a constant reminder so I could be certain to return it on time. The day before I was to return it, I thought, *I'd better at least read enough to let him know I kept my commitment to him.* I picked up the book and started to read. I read an hour, a second hour. I could hardly stop. I read late into the night. It is one of the greatest books I have ever read.

The next day on the way to Harlingen I decided I had to have the book. I was unable to make contact with the loaner; so I gave the book to one of my missionaries and asked him to return it. I said, "Tell him I want to buy it from him. I will give him twenty-five dollars or even fifty dollars, but I must have the book."

The elder returned the book to the owner and carried my message. Then he wrote to me and said that Brother Allred said that it was not for sale.

The next time I saw this good brother I said to him, "I must have that book. I will give you a hundred dollars for it."

He said, "It is the only copy I have and it is not for sale. However, I will try to find you a copy." It was printed in 1882 by the U.S. Publishing House. Hope was dim that I might ever get a copy.

About three months later I was attending a stake conference in McAllen, Texas. Brother Allred came up to me and handed me a sack. He said, "This is a gift for you." I opened the sack and looked in. There was a copy of *Happy Homes and the Hearts That Make Them*. I could not have been more pleased. It had taken him three months and then his son found a copy in a small bookstore in a small community in Eastern Michigan.

I asked, "How much do I owe you for getting me a copy?"

He said, "Nothing. I want you to have this. My son paid for it, and he didn't tell me how much because he wanted to give it to you." Then he continued, "You have published two books. Would you please send him an autographed copy of each of them?"

I could not believe my good fortune. I would have given him ten copies of each of my books for that one volume. Of course, he knew that; but he was interested in a different reward, the pleasure of giving.

Why was I so impressed with this book? I found in it some great pearls of truth that I have never read elsewhere. When I read a book I make notations of things that impress me on the inside cover. My copy of this book has such notations as this: happiness, pages 11, 12, 13; husband's expectation, page 17; woman's importance to man, pages 18, 93, 95, 116; character and genius, page 59; story of Joseph Corbett's mother, page 56; like President Kimball, page 71; Washington's reputation, pages 76, 80, 102; great workers, great thinkers, pages 79, 170, 180; men not to be conquered, page 86; Sir Walter Scott, page 515; and many more. Some of you may recall that this volume was often referred to and quoted in "The Spoken Word," by Richard L. Evans.

Reading opens doors, thoughts, ideas, fantasies, experiences, and it increases knowledge and understanding. Through the masterful writings of those who share their minds through books I have been lifted vicariously to great heights and have experienced the dramatic mentally as if I were physically doing the things about which I was reading.

Books transport us vicariously to every conceivable corner of this abundant creation of God that we call earth. They give us opportunities to probe the minds of the greatest thinkers in all of history. Books excite our emotions to high levels. As I read and reread *Les Misérables*, by Victor Hugo, many emotions filled my breast. I wept as I suffered with the "little ones" who were so cruelly mistreated. I rejoiced and sorrowed on a constantly shifting basis. I felt heroism, inner conflict, turmoil, strength, courage, terror, and faith with each chapter. The translated version I have is about 1,220 pages. The first time I read it I committed myself to read forty pages each night so that I could finish in thirty days. I kept that commitment. Then I read it twice more and still read in it regularly. What a loss I would have suffered if I had not kept my full commitment to read the entire book.

I love good books and I love the men who have taken the time to write them. Some of my most glorious experiences have come from reading. Oh, what rest, what exquisite joy to be transported to the greatest experiences of adventure, spirit, greatness, love, mercy, and charity through good books!

Books are very precious. I can count thousands of hours of pleasure and inspiration they have given me. They are drink and food when the pressures of a busy life have drained my spiritual energies and have left me with a thirst that milk cannot quench and with a hunger that honey cannot satisfy. I have feelers out for new and precious volumes that are coming on the market, and I listen to the people I admire and respect to hear the titles of the classics they have read in the past. I have bought as many books as I could and have thus accumulated about two thousand volumes, a great number of which I have read.

Malcolm Muggeridge, in *The End of Christendom,* tells a story that illustrates the nurture of books. He went to visit a wizened, old, blind bushman in Darwin, Australia. This man had heard Muggeridge on the radio from his hospital bed and had asked for a visit. Muggeridge was deeply touched and searched his mind desperately for something to say to cheer him. Suddenly he remembered what Gloster said to the old man in *King Lear:* "I stumbled when I saw." As Muggeridge left the ward, he could hear the poor old man repeating the words over and over: "I stumbled when I saw." He had heard with his ears, his heart, and his mind. Muggeridge concluded the story with this comment: "That is what I mean by the marvelous power of words when they are used with true force in their true meaning." (Grand Rapids: William B. Eerdmans Publishing Company, 1980, page 3.)

I think of the need to read as a dual commitment: first, the commitment to read on a regular basis; and second, the commitment to learn from the "great trees in the forest," the patriarchs who have wisdom to shed upon us in as great abundance as the leaves falling to the earth in the autumn. We may have to search for the great books. They are not always the popular ones. They are not always those that are honored by the famous and the learned. If our standards are the standard works, we will develop the values that will help us find the best books.

I think that the height of a patriarch in the forest of authors can best be measured by the growth he generates or the light he sheds on the reader. This growth must be so lasting that it serves as well in the next life as it does in this. The light must be eternal or it is darkness instead of light. I would like to fortify this idea in the words of Og Mandino. In his book *The Greatest Salesman in the World* he said this:

> Today I am born anew and my birthplace is a vineyard where there is fruit for all.
> Today I will pluck grapes of wisdom from the tallest and fullest vines in the vineyard, for these were planted by the wisest of my profession who have come before me, generation upon generation.
> Today I will savor the taste of grapes from those vines and verily I will swallow the seed of success buried in each and new life will sprout within me. (New York: Frederick Fell Publishers, Inc., 1968, pages 57-58.)

The faithful know that the tallest vines in the vineyard are the prophets and apostles of all ages, especially their words that are preserved in holy writ. We can learn wisdom as we apply the teachings and principles they share. There may be some others as good and wise; but remember the endowment the prophets and apostles have by the laying on of hands which sets them apart to their high calling, one part of which is the dispensing of the wisdom that comes directly from God by new revelation.

There are many books available. We can select from them as we please. Each book contains a philosophy or thought that the author is desirous of sharing. It may well be his or her greatest thinking on the subject. Undoubtedly the author has intense feelings or he or she would not have taken precious time to write the book. But we must have true Christian standards to guide us in our selections. Our time is precious, too. It would take many lifetimes to read all the books; and many are best left untouched.

Elder Sterling W. Sill in his own books has suggested many of the books that I have purchased and read. Many books about which he has written have become my favorite possessions and companions. The list would include *Bunker Bean, A Fortune to*

Share, Acres of Diamonds, much of the Harvard Classics, *The Magnificent Obsession, The Man Without a Country, The Other Wiseman, Disputed Passage, Sohrab and Rustum, Ivanhoe, Uncle Tom's Cabin,* and many more. When I served as a stake president, Elder Sill visited our stake. What a marvelous two days of training and teaching! As he left to return to Salt Lake, one of our bishops said, "It was like trying to force all the wisdom and knowledge of years through the small end of a funnel. It was all there. It just couldn't come out fast enough." His love of books had a great deal of influence on what he became. And so it can with you if you love the right books.

Read great books. Associate vicariously or in reality with men and women of character and integrity. Rub shoulders with them. Probe into their mental recesses and stretch yourself to a new dimension. You will never be the same. With each experience you will become a larger person, more nearly like those with whom you associate through reading. Commit now to read uplifting literature and great books every day while always reading the scriptures on a daily basis.

Commitments to read regularly can be a great help to the spiritual and intellectual development of most people; but the amount of time or the number of pages will vary from person to person if wisdom prevails. There are people who make emotional commitments that are unrealistic and impossible to keep. Also, we vary a great deal in nervous and physical stamina. Some need eight hours minimum sleep every night or they get sick. All these variables have to be taken into account.

I guess every mission president can tell you how missionaries come in and sit in front of them and say, "President, I've been doing some thinking and I heard what you said at conference and I'm going to improve. I'm going to do this and this and this." And you are aware that some of them may not be using good judgment; because they said that the time before and the time before that. But they *want* to. Of course, most of them do keep their commitments.

I want to suggest something to you: Don't make a commitment that you don't keep. If you have decided on January first that you are going to read the Bible by April first, keep that commitment or don't make it. You can harm your character by making commitments you don't keep. It can become a habit, an ingrained characteristic. You are telling your subconscious mind that it is all right to make all these promises and then not keep them. By and by the subconscious begins to feed back a negative feeling. It tells you that you are a failure and never keep your promises to yourself. The longer this goes on, the harder it is to undo the damage. It would have been better to have stayed satisfied with yourself as you were.

Drop it down and say, "I'm only going to read one page a day," or some amount that you know is possible, reasonable, and in line with your other time demands. Then *do* it. Don't ever set an unreasonable goal that you can't keep. The size or difficulty of the commitment is really critical. I've seen this in men and women in and out of the Church. Great people everywhere seem to have an ability to commit to something and then really get it done. The idea is to push yourself, but not so much that you set up a failure pattern. If you are going to commit to read the scriptures fifteen minutes a day, do it, and never violate that commitment. Maybe a verse a day or a one minute commitment is all you can make to start with. Very few people are able to keep a commitment of an hour of reading a day. Such a commitment usually means failure. So be practical.

I had a great blessing as a young man. I read Elder Sterling W. Sill's first leadership book. When I finished the chapter "Twice Born Men," which is toward the end of the book, it so affected me that I went downstairs and knelt down and prayed for a long time. I was never the same after that. I came back up to bed an hour or so later, and I just wasn't the same. I was a different person. I had made a commitment that I was going to read. I credit my reading with supplying more of my education than any time I spent in school. And I find this is generally true among truly educated people: They have learned more from the great books they have read than from their formal education.

I decided I was going to read every night a certain period of time. I knew that if I was going to read the books that are commonly recommended and, on top of that, read the scriptures every day, it would take a strong commitment. Therefore, I made a commitment that has become a habit. No matter what time I get the duties of the day finished, I read my committed allotment of time in something like *Les Misérables,* or *Uncle Tom's Cabin,* or *A Tale of Two Cities* — the great classics. Then I always conclude by reading out of the scriptures. I can't tell you the reading that I have been able to accomplish through the years just by doing that one thing: keeping that commitment to myself. I commend that to you. Even a minute a day is enough to finish a fair-sized book in a year. That is more serious reading than most mature people accomplish. But whatever you do, do not commit to something you can't or won't do. And, of course, pick the time of day that suits your schedule and personality. For some it may be the first thing in the morning. Some use their lunch hour.

After Jesus' resurrection, he appeared several times to various witnesses chosen beforehand, foremost among whom were the apostles. On the occasion that John calls "the third time that Jesus shewed himself to his disciples" (John 21:14), Jesus pressed Peter very hard to make a commitment to feed Jesus' sheep. Three times he asked Peter, "Lovest thou me?" Twice Peter answered, "Yea, Lord; thou knowest that I love thee." The third time, being "grieved" at Jesus' repetition of the question, Peter answered, "Lord, thou knowest all things; thou knowest that I love thee." (John 21:15-17.)

Then Jesus made this significant prophecy:

> Verily, verily, I say unto thee, When thou wast young, thou girdedst thyself, and walkedst whither thou wouldest: but when thou shalt be old, thou shalt stretch forth thy hands, and another shall gird thee, and carry thee whither thou wouldest not.
>
> This spake he, signifying by what death he should glorify God. And when he had spoken this, he saith unto him, Follow me. (John 21:18-19.)

Adam Clarke, in his famous commentary on the Old and New Testaments, made the following observation on these verses:

> Wetstein observes that it was a custom at Rome to put the necks of those who were to be crucified into a yoke, and to *stretch out their hands* and fasten them to the end of it; and having thus led them through the city they were carried out to be crucified. . . . Thus then Peter was girded, chained, and carried *whither he would not*—not that he was unwilling to die for Christ; but he was a *man* —he did not *love death*; but he loved his *life less* than he loved his God. . . .
>
> Ancient writers state that, about thirty-four years after this [After Jesus' prophecy], Peter was crucified; and that he deemed it so *glorious* a thing to die for Christ that he begged to be crucified with his *head downwards*, not considering himself worthy to die in the same posture in which his Lord did. So [wrote] *Eusebius, Prudentius, Chrysostom,* and *Augustin.* (*Clarke's Commentary,* Matthew to Revelation [Nashville: Abingdon, n.d.], page 663. Italics as in the original.)

I hope none of us have to go as far as Peter had to go to keep our commitments; but we should be willing to when the commitments are good. We should make them small enough so that we can surely keep them. Then we will not be fragmenting the fabric of our character. Then as our character grows, our commitments can be larger and harder. That is what is meant by learning to walk before you run.

A recent reading experience deeply affected my family life. My sons had been after me to read *The Hobbit* and *The Lord of the Rings* (3 volumes) by J. R. R. Tolkien. Since my reading time is limited, I am very selective and try to read only at my highest interest or greatest pleasure level. I have always loved adventure and exploration books; but I thought something like Tolkien's works might be a little too much on the fantasy or science-fiction side for my purposes. I came later to the realization that Professor Tolkien was more of a philosopher, perhaps, than a storyteller. Though he certainly was a great storyteller. Those who have pursued him even as far as the *Silmarillion* are aware that his stories have the roots of eternity in them. There are shadows of the war in heaven, a fallen angel of light, fallen men, degrees of intelligences, and possibly even the wanderings of the lost tribes of Israel. Of course, most of it seems to be based on pagan mythology. Like all the ancient legends and myths, it tends to verify the biblical account of a world tortured by great cataclysms and wars that devastate whole lands and peoples. Accompanying everything else, there is the thread of tragedy. If you have wept over David, you will weep over Feanor.

Perhaps all those who read this are not aware that Professor Tolkien's books—at least *The Hobbit* and the trilogy—are must reading in many secondary and college reading lists for literature courses. J. R. R. Tolkien was a professor of Anglo-Saxon at Oxford University for twenty years and then occupied the Merton endowed English languages and literature professorial chair there for the fourteen years before his retirement. Tolkien's several books have sold upwards of forty million copies. *The Hobbit* and each volume of the trilogy or *The Lord of the Rings* had sold eight million copies by 1981, a total of over thirty-two million copies for these four most popular of Tolkien's books. He died in 1973 having received much acclaim. But his fame after death has far exceeded anything he knew in life.

My sons pressed me to read Tolkien's four most popular books, and I felt an obligation to do it so that we could discuss them together. As soon as I gave in and commenced reading, my sons started getting excited. As a family we have told and retold the stories, adventures, and intimate experiences of Frodo, Gandalf and Arathorn. The hours we have spent excitedly discussing these books were worth every moment of time it took to read them.

I read the trilogy in about forty days, a task of about fifteen hundred pages. It was an adventure. There was nothing degrading. Right and truth triumphed in the end. Tolkien is a magnificent artist who paints pictures with words. With great talent he expresses his creative imagination as skillfully as anyone I have ever read. A steady, constant commitment to good twines itself like a golden thread from chapter to chapter and book to book.

There are many side benefits from keeping our commitments to self-improvement through reading, participating in cultural experiences, writing, studying scriptures, praying and exercising daily, and so forth. Most everyone believes in all of these things, but few actually do them. Those who make a commitment to self-improvement realize the initial blessings and the side benefits, as my reading of Tolkien illustrates. These side benefits are many, but better human relations lead the way.

There is one more thought that I would like to pursue before leaving this idea of the value of books. The Bible has been called the Book of Books and many other ennobling titles. Some of the world's greatest thinkers have said that Job is the greatest, the most sublime, piece of literature ever penned. Others have said that David was the most gifted musician and psalmist of all time. Moses was the greatest law giver. Until humanism conquered our courts and law schools, the Bible, especially Moses, was consulted as the last authority in the field of law. Paul was hailed as the master theologian and missionary. And through it all, the Shepherd of Israel, the Christ of Christendom, was the source of Job's, Moses', David's, and Paul's inspiration. Jehovah's infinite mind gave the writers of the Bible the words that have set fire to the very inside of the bones of hundreds of millions who have read them. (Jeremiah 20:9.) Untold thousands have given their lives for the Bible. It has floated down to you through the centuries on a river of blood. How precious to you is this book that has been bought so dearly?

The Communists in Russia set out to crush the Bible and Christianity. But they have failed. Prisoners in Siberia carry scraps of paper in their pockets on which are copied choice passages from the Gospels. They survive by reading these passages when they can. They not only survive, they are changed dramatically into kind and gracious Christians. Think of the power of the words of this book, the Bible!

Muggeridge testifies further to the power of the books of the great Tolstoy. He tells how in an interview with Anatoli Kusnyetsov, another Soviet Christian writer, he asked Kusnyetsov how he came about his Christian orientation. Kusnyetsov said "that Stalin made one fatal error: he neglected to suppress the works of Tolstoy." Had Stalin been more of a reader — at least of great and good books — he would have know that Tolstoy's books were filled with Christianity and perpetuated much of the Bible's thought and inspiration. This explains — at least in part — the fact that Russian officials admit that as many as 30 percent of their people are still "believers." (Malcolm Muggeridge, *The End of Christendom,* pages 44-46.)

Thus some of the best books are preparing a people for a great missionary work and harvest that awaits us. And it is not only in Russia where this is happening. Besides the influence of the Bible, there are cases here and there about the world where copies of the Book of Mormon have converted whole congregations before a missionary ever was seen.

Such are the profound influences of the written word, not just of the scriptures but of Christ-oriented writers in the great literature. Besides the Christian influence there is much of value, especially in the pursuit of scientific knowledge and other useful information, in the great works of other honest and capable thinkers. If you haven't begun to enrich your life by reading, perhaps it is time to dig for this treasure by making some kind of a reading commitment, be it great or small.

5

Turning Bad Things Into Good With Courage

There was a minister down in Harlingen, Texas, who was pretty critical of the elders. He would watch for them on the street and then slip up behind them and say, "Are you wearing your secret underwear?" He did this over and over. The elders were offended, befuddled, and embarrassed. They didn't know how to handle it. What made matters worse, this minister was a big intimidating man—about six foot five and 260 pounds. His father also was a minister. They had a little printing press and some other business.

One day this big minister saw a new elder, Elder Cornet, and his companion in the post office as they were in line waiting to buy some stamps. He walked up behind this new victim and said, "Do you have your secret underwear on?" Elder Cornet looked shocked as he turned around and looked at this stranger. Then he backed off and in a voice loud enough for everyone in the post office to hear said, "Man, what kind of a weirdo are you, asking about my underwear?" All of a sudden all the attention was on this man, and he turned red and walked out of the post office. You would have to know Elder Cornet to fully appreciate this. He was a convert of only about a year when he went on his mission and had had the kind of background that gave him this sort of presence of mind.

I felt a responsibility and desire to interview this minister; so I went down to Harlingen to see him. I took off my mission president identification button and put it in my pocket. I had the elders drop me off at the corner near where he lived. I went down the street and knocked on his door. His wife came to the door, and I asked to see her husband, the pastor. She said he was across the street in the printing plant in his father's home. I asked if I could go over and see him. She not only said I could but she took me right over and into the house. I probably wouldn't have gotten in if she hadn't been there. The old minister was in a wheelchair, and as he looked at me I felt that he suspected something was amiss.

He started wheeling over toward me and said, "Who did you say you were?"

I said, "I'm Vaughn Featherstone. I used to work in Boise for the Albertson's food centers. I was the corporate training director up there."

He heaved a sign of relief and said, "Well, come in and sit down."

"Thank you." I sat down and said, "I'd just like to tell you a little more. Four years ago I was called by the First Presidency of The Church of Jesus Christ of Latter-day Saints to be a member of the Presiding Bishopric of that church."

"Well, you can get out of my home. If I had known who you were, you wouldn't have been allowed to come into it."

I said, "I know that. That is why I didn't tell you. But I want to just say this much to you. . . ." Then we started talking.

He asked, "Do you believe in Christ?"

I said, "Of course we do."

He then asked, "Do you believe in God the Father?"

I said, "We certainly do."

He went on asking other questions and then he asked, "Do you believe that Jesus Christ and God the Eternal Father are separate?"

I said, "Of course they are."

"Then get out of my house."

This was the second time he had asked me to leave and I just sat there. Of course, his son (six foot five, about 260 pounds) was in the other room. But he wasn't all that lean and all that hard; so I was not intimidated—yet at least. So I said to him, very much like Paul on the way to Damascus, "The Lord would call you to do a great work here. I have a message for you just as surely as the Lord had a message for Paul." Then I told him what he could do if he would listen to us and let us take him through the discussions.

He said, "I won't do it. I'm not interested. I know you are messengers of the devil."

Then I asked them if they would read the Book of Mormon.

He said, "We've got one, but we won't read it."

I asked, "Will you read one chapter or just one page?"

"I won't touch it."

I turned to the son who had been asking about the secret underwear and asked, "Will you read it?"

He said, "Well, I'll read some of it."

I asked, "Will you read 3 Nephi?"

He said, "Well . . . okay, I'll read 3 Nephi."

I said, "You're a man of your word, a pastor in Jesus Christ's labor, as you put it, so I would expect you to keep your word. Then, after you have read that book, you will know what to do. You will ask God if it is true."

Then the old man said, "What are you doing here anyway?"

"We have had a problem with your son. He has been walking up behind our elders and criticizing them about the sacred underclothing that we wear. I want you to know that they are sacred. And I can't imagine why, if you profess to be followers of Jesus Christ, you would do that. I can't believe that Jesus or any of his followers would say something so critical about something so sacred to someone else."

This old pastor turned to his son and said, "Did you do that?"

The son looked embarrassed and blushed; but he was on the spot. He said, "Well, I didn't mean any harm." He didn't tell his experience with Elder Cornet in the post office. Neither did I. My only reason for being there was to improve a bad situation. I had no malicious feelings.

Finally, the meeting was just about ended. I had been there about half an hour, which was twenty-nine minutes longer than I was led to hope for at the start. I stood up and bore my testimony to them and said, "One day you will have witness borne to your soul who you have had in your home this day. I am an ambassador of Christ and have been sent to you by his true apostles."

The old one said, "You have not."

"I have and I bear that testimony to you." I told them about Joseph Smith being a prophet and the Book of Mormon being true. Then I reached out to shake hands and the old minister wouldn't shake hands with me. He said it would be like shaking hands with the devil.

I said, "All right, adieu, brethren."

They said, "We're not your brethren."

I said, "Yes you are. You just don't know it yet."

I left and that was it. But I believe that there does come a time when we must stand up to be counted. I think we ought to defend our testimonies. There are times when someone is critical and it is best to ignore it or overlook it. But I have been in many situations where someone has been critical of the Church when I thought it was necessary to stand up and be counted. Someone has said, "Though argument does not change belief, the lack of it destroys belief."

We have had no more problems in Harlingen with those ministers from that day on. They quit criticizing us openly about anything. I believe they had at least some inkling of whom they were speaking with.

Sometimes members and even elders will speculate about how we would feel if missionaries from other churches came to our doors with their message. They make it sound as if we would be facing the same problems in that situation that the people of the world face when our elders come to their doors. Well, if that is the case, then we wouldn't be sending out any missionaries. And, if you believe that, you have no business investing any time or money in missionary work. Either this is the kingdom of God, restored by Gods, angels, and ordained servants of God, or it isn't. If it verily is the kingdom of God, then what God has said is true: The angels go before us and the Spirit bears witness. (D&C 84:62-91, especially verse 88.) And when missionaries from other churches come to our doors, the situation is reversed: The Spirit bears witness that they are not the servants of the Master. But we don't have to tell them that. We can try to tell them the glorious good news we have heard ourselves about the angels who have flown through the midst of heaven and have restored the truths that were lost.

What you have just read represents the faith of this fine young man, Elder Cornet, who fulfilled his mission, went home, and married in the temple. He had been in the Church just a year when he went out. He was one of the greatest of all the elders who came to Texas. One of his strongest points was simply that he feared no man. Like the young David, he believed that God is with the people who have been commissioned by God. He absolutely wasn't afraid of anyone and his work showed that. Very often people do the wrong thing because they haven't the courage to do the right thing.

Commitment, in a large sense, demands self-control of the highest order. Self-control in any form is nothing less than courage. True manhood may never come to an individual until self-control is an integral part of his character. The same can be said for true womanhood, though it generally is conceded that women seem to be naturally endowed with more self-control than men.

> Self control is at the root of all the virtues. Let a man give the reins to his impulses and passions and from that moment he yields up his moral freedom. He is carried along the current of life, and becomes the slave of his strongest desires for the time being.

The most self reliant, self governing man is always under discipline; and the more perfect the discipline, the higher will be his moral condition. He has to drill his desires and keep them in subjection to the higher powers of his nature. They must obey the word of command of the internal monitor, the conscience — otherwise they will be but the mere slaves of their inclinations, the sport of feeling and impulse. (*Happy Homes and the Hearts That Make Them*, Samuel Smiles [Chicago: U.S. Publishing House; 1882], pages 472, 473.)

The Church has taught and continues to instruct us that the greatest seminary of moral discipline is the home. Men and women who demonstrate self-control, frugality, and discipline, and who set examples for their children in these matters are the teachers.

The best regulated home is always that in which the discipline is the most perfect, and yet where it is the least felt. (*Happy Homes and the Hearts That Make Them*, page 474.)

The men who are really men are "gentle" men. In *Defender of the Faith: The B. H. Roberts Story*, Truman G. Madsen quotes B. H. Roberts as follows: "They make no slaves of their women; they make companions of them; and in honoring them they honor themselves." (Salt Lake City: Bookcraft, Inc., 1980, page 96.)

It is a simple matter to judge men. Watch closely how they treat women. Observe carefully their relationship with little children. Make a study of how they respect and deal with other men. The truly great man is noble in relations with all men, all women, and ever so taken up with little children. He attracts, not repels, others.

I read a story about an explorer named George Dawson in a Royal Bank of Canada Newsletter. George Dawson was slight in stature, just over five feet when he was full grown. He had serious respiratory diseases and was not strong. He was an engineer and spent most of his adult life exploring, mapping, and surveying Canada. Winter and summer he labored. He died at a relatively young age of just over fifty. A town that has been immortalized in stories, poetry, and song is named after him. At his funeral they eulogized him in these words:

And tell him the men he worked with
Say, judging as best they can,
That in lands that try manhood the hardest
He was tested and proven a man.

Commitment and self-control are as inseparable as loving brothers. The man or woman who would keep commitments must not be deterred, redirected, or distracted, or become wishy-washy or weak-kneed. Self-control is a great quality that keeps our eyes single to our goals.

I have always loved David, the psalmist. As a boy, I remember reading in the Bible about him. His words as a teenage visitor to the army of Israel thrilled me. On that occasion Goliath, the giant of Gath, had challenged Saul's army daily to send out a single combatant to meet him. The winner was also to win victory for his side of the war. No one had accepted the challenge. Only the teenaged David comprehended the true implications of the situation. He said, "Who is this uncircumcised Philistine, that he should defy the armies of the living god?" (1 Samuel 17:26.)

David's words greatly provoked his oldest brother, Eliab, who said, "Why camest thou down hither? and with whom hast thou left those few sheep in the wilderness? I know thy pride, and the naughtiness of thine heart; for thou art come down that thou mightest see the battle." (1 Samuel 17:28.)

And David replied, "What have I now done? Is there not a cause?" (1 Samuel 17:29.)

He could have defended his position by saying his father had sent him with food. But David now saw a larger cause and was so wrapped up in it that it pervaded his whole mind. He had a heart like unto God's own heart. He had slain a lion and a bear in defense of his father's flocks and rightly discerned that his power was the power of the Lord.

It is very likely that no one much more than hoped that David could succeed. Yet so desperate was Israel's plight—not because of any actual danger, but because of the fear of the wicked who had lost their faith—that even the king, a great warrior in his own right, accepted David's offer to meet Goliath. David must have been a good-sized lad; he did not refuse Saul's armor because it was too big, but because he had not learned to fight in such trappings. And Saul was head and shoulders above all Israel in his youth. (1 Samuel 9:2.) But it was in the heart of David where his strength lay. When he went out to meet Goliath, he answered Goliath's insulting taunt with these words that probably have inspired and thrilled more godly and brave souls than any other words ever spoken:

> Thou comest to me with a sword, and with a spear, and with shield: but I come to thee in the name of the Lord of hosts, the God of the armies of Israel, whom thou has defied.
>
> This day will the Lord deliver thee into mine hand; and I will smite thee, and take thine head from thee; and I will give the carcases of the host of the Philistines this day unto the fowls of the air, and to the wild beasts of the earth; that all the earth may know that there is a God in Israel.
>
> And all this assembly shall know that the Lord saveth not with sword and spear: for the battle is the Lord's and he will give you into our hands. (1 Samuel 17:45-47.)

Then David did not go forward with shaking legs and cautious step. His strength was not vitiated by assailing doubts. But he "hasted, and ran toward the army to meet the Philistine." (1 Samuel 17:48.) Mind you, it was not Goliath alone who stood out there in front of him. There was a large army with a wall of spears and swords pointed in his direction. Thousands of arrows were notched and ready. Because as soon as David fell, the Philistines would pour down the hillside, across the vale, and up into the cringing ranks of the Israelites. As David went forward as fast as he could run, he was fitting a stone into his sling, a very round one that he had selected from the brook over which he had crossed. When he was near enough, he whirled the sling around his head and released the stone. It sank into Goliath's forehead, and he fell to the ground with a crash. David then severed the giant's head with Goliath's own sword. I can imagine that he held it up for all Israel to see. Consternation swept the ranks of the Philistines, and the Israelites remembered who they were. Then all of David's prophecy to Goliath was fulfilled and a very bad situation was made good by courage and commitment.

David became the standard by which God judged all other kings, and none measured up to him in the conduct of his duty as king—in his fairness as a judge, and in his generosity to his associates and to the downtrodden. But David's commitment was not complete. At least it wavered in regard to his personal life. We do not know his ultimate fate; but we do know that he was both a great positive and negative example, but at different times, to which we often look for guidance.

It is not uncommon for the Saints, like David, to be more willing to do the dramatic things than the day by day common, ordinary heroics that usually are not called heroics. Brigham Young said that more Saints are willing to die for the Church than live for it. When I think of day by day quiet heroics, I think most of all mothers. In our day especially it takes courage to be a mother.

A daughter of a leader in one of our stakes announced, "I am not going to have any children."

Her father said, "What?"

She repeated, "I'm not going to have any children. Don't you know that there is a zero population campaign and we should not have any children? What's more, we have four in our family already and I would appreciate it if you wouldn't have any more. I am embarrassed to go to school and feel the pressure there. I am simply a political outcast because we have four children in our family."

Now, that illustrates an attitude that unfortunately has even crept into the thinking of some of the daughters of Zion. By contrast let me tell you another story. A little mother back East who was expecting her fifth child went in to see a doctor. They had just moved back there, and she asked him to be her obstetrician and he said he would be glad to. They started filling out a case history, and as they got down to children, he asked, "How many children do you have?"

She said, "This will be our fifth."

He gasped and said, "What do you mean? You have four and are expecting your fifth? I had better not treat you during your pregnancy. What we had better do is have an abortion performed. I will make the arrangements. You are way over the limit right now with four children. You surely do not want any more. By the way, how many children were you planning on having?"

This woman stood up, but before she walked out of his office she said, "At least thirty-five."

God bless her. I tell you, when people tell a righteous Saint one thing and God says another, it doesn't set well. Our faithful sisters wouldn't care if they were beaten to death. If God tells them to have children, they will have them. Never mind what Darwin, Malthus, and Women's Lib say. Our mothers want to stand in the liberty that makes them free, and that is the liberty of obedience to God. But, brethren, they don't need to be compelled to be obedient in this manner. Having a baby is a choice blessing and a wondrous gift. So it ought to be voluntary. Besides, most of your wives will have as many babies voluntarily as they would under righteous persuasion. So let them feel happy about it.

Looking at it from the standpoint of worldly philosophy, having babies might be called a bad thing. Of course, it isn't. It is a beautiful thing. But it is a great trial. Through courage, however, all good women turn this great physical trial into good.

The Book of Mormon is rich in stories about missionaries who turned bad situations into good by courage. The first half of the book of Alma is especially rich in these stories. There we read about Ammon and his brethren who asked to go among the Lamanites to preach the gospel. It was a very dangerous assignment. They were in danger of arrest, imprisonment, and execution daily. Yet they converted thousands of souls. And it was because of their courage. Read again the story of Ammon, who was bound and brought before the king in the land of Ishmael. This king could do as he pleased with Ammon — kill him, enslave him, or set him free. Ammon asked only to be a servant of the king, who was so pleased with Ammon's deport- ment and courage that he gave him his wish. Later Ammon's courageous defense of the king's flocks led to an opportunity to teach the gospel to the king and many of his people. This, in turn, led to other great teaching experiences and courageous deeds.

Joseph, the son of Jacob, is another example of courage in the face of adversity. You recall that Joseph was sold by his brothers and was taken into a foreign land, the land of Egypt. In those days that may as well have been halfway round the world. Anyway, Joseph arrived in Egypt a slave and ended up in the household staff of Potiphar. But he didn't pout and cringe and feel sorry for himself. He worked hard and served well. It was not long until he was second only to Potiphar. He had made a bad situation into a good one by courage and optimism. But there was worse to come.

Potiphar's wife fell in love with Joseph. Joseph was a very good-looking man. Women were deeply affected by his beauty of body and soul. In one version of an interesting tradition, Potiphar's wife, having been criticized for her love for Joseph, invited forty of the ladies of the court to see for themselves. She gave them knives and oranges to cut and called for Joseph. When they saw him, they were so amazed at his beauty that their hands all slipped and they all cut themselves and exclaimed, "O . . .! This is not a human being, this is none other than a glorious angel!" (Adam Clarke, *Clarke's Commentary,* Genesis to Esther, page 228.) In another version, they were all sewing and jabbed themselves with their needles when they saw Joseph. How Potiphar stayed in the dark is not explained in these tradi- tions.

Finally, Potiphar's wife was so overcome with lust that she tried to force her attentions on Joseph. Joseph's reply to her pleadings was a classic that has been an inspiration to the righ- teous ever since: "How then can I do this great wickedness, and sin against God?" The scriptural account says that ". . . he left his garment in her hand, and fled, and got him out." (Genesis 39:9, 12.) There are no end of people who would be better off in this world and especially the next if they had "got them out" of temptation while they still could. But it didn't fare well with Joseph in the short run. Potiphar's wife changed the details of the story and used Joseph's cloak as proof that he had tried to seduce her. Potiphar believed the lie and Joseph spent several years in prison.

Did Joseph spend his time in prison cursing his luck and his Maker? Not on your life. He went to work and became the chief trustee of the prison. God was with him and he prospered. He even was blessed with the powers of the Spirit so that he interpreted dreams. I can imagine that he preached the gospel to whomever would listen. But he did not neglect his duties. Like Ammon, he served his master well. And this led to another great experience. Eventually, he turned this bad thing into such a good thing that he became the savior of all his people Israel. Because of his suffering and his service, he is used sometimes as a prototype of Christ. He became a king in Egypt, second only to the Pharaoh. All power was given to him in Egypt to do as he pleased. And we know of no case in which he misused that power.

I suppose if we took a test right now and asked the readers if they have been effective in missionary work or if they are doing what they ought to be doing in missionary work, most would think they haven't measured up. I think for some reason there is something in the Church that makes us feel guilty that we are not doing enough. No matter how much we do, we are made to feel it is too little. But maybe you are better off than you think. If we asked how many of you are living a good life, an exemplary life, everyone could say yes most of the time. If we asked how many are supporting or have supported missionaries in the field, nearly everyone could respond affirmatively. How many subscribe to the *New Era* or *Ensign* for other people? Many do. We could go down the list of missionary responsibilities and about the only thing you are not doing is actual proselyting or getting missionaries into the homes of your friends. Most of you probably aren't holding cottage meetings quite the way you should and maybe could. But really, you are 99 percent missionaries, and I think you ought to feel good about that. We do not want you to feel guilty. We just want you to go that one extra little turn and introduce your friends to missionaries. Some of you claim that you don't want the missionaries to go to your friends because the missionaries aren't capable enough to teach your friends. J. Golden Kimball is reported to have said, "I know this Church is true, or the missionaries would have ruined it long ago." There are some unprepared missionaries; but most of them can handle whatever comes along if they have courage. And if you are "smart" enough to think the missionaries can't handle it, that puts an even greater burden on you: You had better get busy and do it yourself so it will be done right.

But with most of us the thing that is holding us back is that we do not have the courage to ask our friends to let us send the missionaries over. It reminds me of the woman who went in to get her boy up for school, and she said to him, "You've got to go."

He said, "I'm not going to go today."

She said, "You have to go."

He said, "I won't go."

Finally, she put a little pressure on him and said, "You are going to go. You give me two good reasons why you're not going to go."

He said, "In the first place, all the students hate me and in the second place all the teachers hate me. Now, you give me two good reasons why I should go."

She said, "In the first place, you are forty-four years old and in the second place you are the principal."

I suppose that is it. Members are all principals, and we need to get up and do something courageous about missionary work and everything else we may be shirking. And the only thing wrong with telling that is that the ones who didn't need to hear it will feel guilty and the ones who did need to hear it might know where the valve is that turns off the guilty juices.

When I was a mission president I went down to McAllen, Texas, and met a wonderful family after Sunday School. Elder Brown said to me, "President, I want you to meet this family, Brother and Sister Gutierrez and their four adult children. Three of them are school teachers and three of them are going to be baptized today." Then he told me which were going to be baptized.

I said, "What about the rest of you?"

They said, "Well, we are not ready yet."

So I talked to them for a minute, bore my testimony, and then put my arm around Brother Gutierrez, this old, hard, Mexican father who had worked all his life. He had rough, gnarled hands which had supported his children all the way through high school and college. They were respected in the community and were making a real contribution. I put my arm around him and said, "Brother Gutierrez, one day you and this good woman will kneel across the altar in a holy temple and you will be sealed together for all eternity. These four grown sons and daughters will be dressed in white clothing as you will be, and you will be sealed as a forever family by someone who has authority. I know that will take place. Please read the Book of Mormon and pray about it. Ask God if this book is true and ask him if Joseph Smith really was a prophet." Then I left and went out. It was right after meeting.

You would have to see the McAllen chapel to fully appreciate the rest of the story. It is about the normal size; but it has a special front made of uniformly large rocks that the members picked up for that purpose. It is very beautiful, really magnificent. And there is a wide and spectacular walkway between the stake offices, the chapel, and the cultural hall. There are palm trees on each side of the walkway. They keep the lawn just manicured, and it is a beautiful place for people to come to. To me, at least, it is the most elegant and beautiful church house of any denomination in the McAllen area.

After meeting the Gutierrez family, I went out to get into the car to take my wife over to the bishop's. Elder Brown went into the baptism and then he came running out before we left and he looked like he had something to say. So I said, "Elder Brown, what can I do for you?"

He said, "Nothing," and shook hands.

I said, "Good."

He stood there and I said, "Are you sure there is nothing I can do for you?"

He said, "Yes, I'm sure."

He stood there and I said, "Do you have a place to eat dinner?" I thought maybe he didn't have any place and wanted to eat with us.

He said, "Yes."

So I got into the car and said, "All right, Elder Brown, we'll see you." And he kind of just stood there as we took off. We got about half way to the bishop's house and I said to my wife, "Now I know what Elder Brown was trying to say. I've got to go back."

I took her to the bishop's, turned around and went back. There were a few cars parked there, no one outside. At least, I didn't think there was.

I climbed out of the car, walked down the long, beautiful walk; and I saw the most pitiful, forlorn figure I have ever seen in my life. Sitting alongside the big planter box in front of the McAllen Stake Center was Brother Gutierrez. When I was within ten feet of him, the door opened and Elder Brown came out and saw me. Tears came to his eyes. He didn't say anything but turned and walked back inside.

So I sat down by Brother Gutierrez and said, "Brother Gutierrez, you know that The Church of Jesus Christ of Latter-day Saints is the true church, don't you?"

He said that he did.

"You know that the Book of Mormon is true?"

He said, "I know that."

I said, "You know Joseph was a prophet, don't you?"

He said, "Yes, I do."

I said, "Why aren't you in there being baptized with your family?"

This great old man stood up, looked up at our chapel, and said, "This is a magnificent church. I have got to go out and find another job so I can afford to belong to it."

I sat down with him again and told him about a scroungy little kid who had to wear nurse's shoes to church, an inactive father, a mother who wasn't a member of the Church at that time. I told him what the Church had done for me. I told him that the cost of belonging to the Lord's Church is always the same to every soul and is as easy or hard whether rich or poor. It depends on the state of the soul of each convert. In three parables the Savior illustrated this. He told how a certain man found a treasure hidden in a field and he sold all that he had and bought the field. He also said that the king of heaven is likened unto a goodly merchant, who, finding a pearl of great price, sold all that he had and purchased the pearl. Jesus also likened the kingdom of heaven unto a fisher's net which is cast into the sea. It brings forth of every kind. The good are placed in vessels and the rest are cast off. Then I said to him, "The price is always and everlastingly will be the same for you, for me, for the wealthiest man in the Church. It always is the same. It simply is all we have and nothing less."

The truth of the matter is that everything belongs to the Lord. We are only the stewards of his wealth; and he has a lot more to say about what portion he gives us than we like to think. Some may be rich in lands and goods but poor in talents and gifts. Others may be rich in talents and gifts and poor in land and goods. But they all have to give freely of what they have to build up the kingdom. Then they are rich indeed; because their riches, in a sense, follow them. They can take it with them. We must have the courage to tell that to our contacts so that they understand the terms of God's great covenant of salvation and exaltation. And they must have the courage to accept that doctrine. When they do, they can go from the worst of worlds to the best of worlds.

6

When Wisdom Dictates
a Change of Commitment

As the astronauts went to and from the moon, their direction had to be corrected from time to time. Thus, while it would have appeared to the human eye that the Apollo was traveling in a straight line, its course was really a sort of a zigzag. Our lives, even at best, are somewhat like that. We have to make constant corrections as we pursue with determination the short- and long-range goals to which we are committed. One reason for that is that we sometimes find that some short-range goal has taken us off course to the long-range goal. We may even find that a long-range goal no longer suits us. When we change it, many short-range goals may have to be dropped because they do not help us progress toward the new long-range goal.

Sometimes we even find that we have been impractical in the choice of a goal and we are unable to reach it because of circumstances beyond our control. For instance, we may have pitted our wills against someone with a stronger will, as did a man I heard of once. This fellow thought his wife ought to serve him. He felt it should be a goal of a good marriage for the wife to wait on the husband and make him feel good. So he went home from work one day and announced this plan to his wife.

She sounded agreeable so he laid out the routine. She was to meet him in the hallway when he came home; take him into the living room; seat him in the big easy chair; take off his shoes; put on his slippers; bring him the evening paper; and then crown this whole event by bringing in a nice, tall, cool lemonade. The next night he came home and waited in the hallway and nothing happened. He went into the living room; sat down; took off his shoes himself; slipped his slippers on; went in and got the newspaper; and a while later went out to the kitchen and got a nice, tall, cool lemonade.

While he was in the kitchen, he said to his wife, "Remember what we talked about yesterday?"

She said, "I remember."

"Didn't you think that was a good idea?"

"I thought it was a good idea."

So he thought she just forgot.

The next night he came home and stood in the hallway and again nothing happened. So he decided to change his strategy. He decided he would love her into it. When Saturday came she started getting dressed to go to the store. When he started changing his clothes too, she said, "Where are you going?"

He said, "I want to go to the store with you."

When she got over the shock, they went to the store. She thought to herself, *He is here to check and see if I am paying the right amount for things.* But he was a gentleman about everything. He pushed the cart up and down the aisles and they filled it, with not an unkind word said.

She thought, *He will blow his stack when he gets to the checkstand and has to pay the tab.* But the groceries were checked out with no problem. He helped her out to the car. He assisted her into the house. He put the groceries away.

During the next six weeks he was the ideal husband. He helped with the dishes. He put his pants on hangers in the closet, not over the back of the chair in the bedroom. He hit the hamper with his underwear and stockings. He even squeezed the toothpaste at the bottom of the tube. A perfect husband.

Six weeks later, sure enough it happened. Home from work; met in the hall; ushered into the living room; seated in the big easy chair; shoes taken off; slippers placed on; newspaper brought in; and in a little while, a nice, tall, cool lemonade was brought in to climax this great achievement.

Only, instead of him in the chair, it was her.

Of course, the great thing about it was that this was now the way he wanted it. He didn't want it any other way than that. And, if it had worked out the other way, it only should have if that were the way she wanted it. You see, nothing is good that isn't voluntary.

The purpose of that story was not to designate who should wait on whom in a marriage. In some marriages the husband may serve the wife most, and in others it may be the opposite. Nobody should count. While marriage is a contract, none of the details are enforceable in any practical sense. Everything taken has to be given voluntarily or it is spoiled in the taking. But there is so much that can be given in a marriage and there is so much joy in the giving that wise married people concentrate on goals that improve themselves not their spouses.

And that is one rule we must always remember in setting goals: We may set goals to increase our own light and to offer that light to others; but we cannot set goals for others. We only can inspire them to set their own goals. Once we have accepted Christ as our ideal, we have to give up all goals that are based on using compulsion to improve the lives of others or to make a better world. Defensive force by units of government (including the family, which is the basic unit of government) to punish crime or deter foreign aggression is legitimate. But any form of force to bring about positive good or social improvement is offensive force, and it puts you on the side of the powers of darkness. So the long-range goal must be the Christlike ideal, and all short-range goals should be brought into line. (Incidentally, families must not use even defensive force in precisely the way other governmental units may use it. Children are to be disciplined with love and wisdom.)

Sometimes integrity demands that we abandon or change some commitments. This can happen even when the commitment we abandon is a good commitment, though no longer as important as it was when compared to the new commitment that takes its place. Humans can err; but if to be Christlike is always the goal, we will be constantly correcting in the right direction as did the Apollo mission returning to earth.

A marvelous young missionary served locally in one of the Spanish-speaking countries. While he was on his mission his mother ran off with a man, leaving her large family without a parent. There was no father in the home, so the oldest daughter took over the family. Although she was still relatively young, the family seemed to survive well enough so that the missionary was able to remain in the field. One day Robert Burton, a staff member in the Missionary Department, brought me the news that the oldest daughter, who was not a member of the Church, had decided to abandon the family and go away to school.

The missionary contacted his mission president to ask what he should do. He wanted to serve the Lord, but there was no one at home to care for the younger brothers and sisters. He felt he needed to go home and hold his family together. He already had served twenty months as an excellent missionary.

When Brother Burton told me the story and asked for a decision, I could not respond. I was so filled with emotion for this young elder and his family that I sat for several moments trying to control myself as tears welled up in my eyes. The decision was to have him return to his home to support and care for this family that his father and then his mother had abandoned. Although his commitment when he was called on a mission was for twenty-four months, conditions changed and now his commitment had to be modified and turned to the family. There should never be a feeling of guilt or disloyalty when our commitments are changed because integrity and Christian conduct demand it. Of course, every case is unique. That is why priesthood counsel should be sought when callings are involved in a change of commitment.

Sometimes missionaries teach people who are unwilling to accept the restored gospel because of previous commitments that they thought were to Christ. But we encourage them to reconsider. For example, a woman who had been taught the gospel off and on and had known the elders all her life shared a commitment she had made. She promised her father on his deathbed that she would never leave their church. All through the years she resisted the missionaries and kept her commitment to her father. This woman had gained a testimony that Joseph Smith was a prophet, that the Book of Mormon was true, and that The Church of Jesus Christ of Latter-day Saints was the Lord's true Church. However, her commitment to her father plagued her. She felt that she could not break a deathbed promise.

Finally she had a special manifestation. Her father appeared to her and informed her that her family on the other side of the veil were waiting for her to accept the gospel. She immediately was baptized into the Church, feeling free of guilt and worry. This same thing happens many times in almost every mission. Some well-meaning relative gets a commitment from a loved one not to join The Church of Jesus Christ of Latter-day Saints or not to leave his or her present church. Then it takes a special revelation or the persuasion of a particularly inspired missionary to get the commitment changed and the person on the right course.

There is another major factor which those who have made such commitments should consider. Loyalty can be misguided. When someone is blessed with a testimony of Jesus' relationship to this Church, then the course should be clear. The Savior said, "He that loveth father or mother more than me is not worthy of me: and he that loveth son or daughter more than me is not worthy of me." (Matthew 10:37.)

No commitment should be kept if it stands between you and Christ. Some decisions have eternal consequences; and when a commitment is changed for the better, there should be no guilt. It is a change for the better if the change brings the person and his or her family closer to Christ. The new commitment is the one to hold firm. Every soul who walks this earth may gain a testimony of the truthfulness of the gospel. Once that happens, then our absolute and total allegiance must be to our Lord and Savior, Jesus Christ, above family members or anyone else. The commitments we make to him should be our firm and total ones if they have been based on the truth about him and his modern work.

Just after I arrived in Texas I went out to the airport to see Elders Cornet and Gibson off. We were met there by a little convert named Sister Hilcher. She was on crutches because of a crippled leg. Sister Hilcher's son came in with a camera, and they invited us out so she could have her son take some pictures.

When they had taken the pictures, she called me over to the side and said, "I'd like to share something with you. I have always loved and enjoyed people; so when Elder Gibson and his companion came to my home, I wanted these two fine young men to come in. I don't have very many visitors so I didn't mind talking with them. After the third visit I could see that they wanted to baptize me. I told them that as a little girl I wanted to be a Roman Catholic more than anything in the world. I pleaded with my mother to let me join the Catholic Church; but she would not let me. Finally when I was eighteen, I was initiated into the Roman Catholic Church through the ceremonies they use. I told the elders quite clearly, 'I have been a Roman Catholic ever since, and I intend to be a Roman Catholic all the rest of my life. You're welcome to talk to me, but I will not join your church. I intend to be a Roman Catholic.' At this point a clear voice came to me and said, 'But what do you know about it?' I turned to the elders and said to them, 'But what do I know about it?' And they went through the discussions and I joined the Church." Now she was out at the airport seeing Elder Gibson off for home.

At the same time there was a Brother Jackson seeing Elder Gibson off. He said, "Do you remember the day that I told you never to come back again?"

Very quietly Elder Gibson said, "Yes, I remember."

Then, also very quietly, Brother Jackson responded, "Thank God you came back."

We had a solemn assembly in Texas the next August. The First Presidency and others of the Brethren were there. Seated on the first row to pass the sacrament was President Jackson, now the president of his elders quorum. He was passing the sacrament in a solemn assembly. That thrilled me. This glorious experience never could have come to him if he had not had the courage and wisdom to change a commitment that needed changing.

The very essence of missionary work is the business of helping people change commitments of greater or lesser value for the great commitment of following the true Christ in his true Church. Sometimes it takes one approach and sometimes another. The Spirit will provide the special help we need, as the following story illustrates.

A Catholic priest came to a meeting in which I was speaking. He did not wear his priestly robes, but just came in street clothes. About halfway through my talk I felt impressed to bear a testimony directly to him. I just looked right down in the front where he was sitting and said, "I want everyone here to know that when Joseph Smith walked out of the Sacred Grove, he knew more about God, the Eternal Father, and his Son, Jesus Christ, than all of the pastors, all of the ministers, and all of the popes who have ever walked the earth."

That statement struck this priest with great force and eventually had the necessary prompting effect to help get him into the Church. I learned just before I left Texas to return to Salt Lake that he was going to join the Church. We ought to have a testimony and share it with forthrightness when prompted to do so by the Spirit. I could have reasoned with him about all the things the Church has done that are great, and it probably wouldn't have done much good; but a testimony startled him and caused him to think.

I want to share this next story with you because it shows the power of testimony in a special and significant way. Two of our elders went to the home of Bryce Wanless, a man in his early thirties. His wife, Sue, let them in and listened to them and asked them to come back when her husband was there. Bryce told me after his baptism that when the elders returned that night, he noticed that as they gave the discussion they said, "We know," not "We believe" or "We think." They said, "We know this Church is true," and "We know that God does live," and "We know that Jesus Christ has visited the earth in this day."

The elders invited Bryce and his wife to Church on Sunday. They came and sat about a third of the way back in the middle of the center section of the chapel. One of the Primary-age boys was present with his little rubber flipper and his spit wads. Who did he hit on the back of the head but Bryce Wanless? When I heard that I just got sick. But, you know Bryce turned around and looked at them, and later explained to the elders, "It really hurt—not the spit wad; but it hurt that that kind of conduct should take place in the Church when we believed what we were hearing."

But he and his wife went home and they talked about it and they decided that the conduct of the people really didn't make any difference. Bryce said, "We knew what the elders had said was true."

About a year later when I was in Salt Lake for a general conference, I had the privilege of sealing Bryce and Sue and their two children together for time and all eternity in the Salt Lake Temple.

I don't want to leave the impression that converts must have bad experiences or have a hard time changing commitments from churches that "lack the power of godliness" to the one that Jesus called "the only true and living church." (D&C 1:30.) Many people seem to be just waiting for the missionaries to arrive. I would like to tell you about some of these cases because it may help someone decide to go on a mission or help someone decide to commit himself or herself fully to this great work. After all, that is the meaning in Jacob 2:18-19: Before you settle on any other commitments, get a hope in Christ. That is, find the kingdom. A hope in Christ is another way of describing what happens to you when you have the testimony of Jesus. If you have a hope in Christ — that is, if you have found the kingdom — all the other things will come if you seek them for the right purposes. So, again, there is a hierarchy of commitments. Christ is at the top and all else must fall into line with that one so that there is no disharmony.

We had a young missionary couple in Texas, LeRoy Wilcox and his wife, who tracted over thirteen thousand homes and kept track of what happened. It was a very interesting account. At one home a little lady came to the door. They introduced themselves as missionaries from the Church. She said, "You might as well come in. For ten years I have been searching for the true church, and I haven't found it yet. I might as well listen to you."

After they had finished the first discussion, she said, "I have a whole lot of friends and they know that I've been searching for the true church. Every once in a while, almost every month, I get a call from one or the other of them and they say, 'Have you found the true church yet? When you find it, let us know; because we know that you will recognize it.' "

Brother and Sister Wilcox completed the visit with the usual testimony and prayer. As they got up to leave, for some reason Brother Wilcox said, "We want you to know that we have come from far, far away to give you this message."

She looked startled and said, "Did you say far, far away?"

He said, "Yes."

"How far?"

"Over sixteen hundred miles — from Orem, Utah."

She said, "That is far away. You know, about two years ago a woman appeared to me in a dream and she said, 'You will find the true church. Messengers will come from far, far away.' " What a blessing!

Almost that same week the Wilcoxes had another experience wherein they quoted from Moroni 10:4: "And when ye shall receive these things. . . ." They went through the whole passage. When they had finished, the woman they were visiting said, "I have been searching for that scripture. I heard that in a dream. I was told that I would find the truth wherever I would find that scripture. Where is it? Will you let me read it?"

They opened the Book of Mormon, and she read it two or three times. She soon joined the Church.

Down on the Rio Grande a Spanish-speaking elder in our mission went to a home and knocked on the door, and the woman of the house said, "Come in. Maybe you can help me."

They said, "We think we can."

So they went in and said, "What's the problem?"

She replied, "I had a dream. I dreamed last night that there was a man and he met me and took me by the hand and walked with me all the way down to the Rio Grande. Then he walked out into the river and beckoned for me to come out into the river."

They said, "We think we have the answer."

So they started through the first discussion, and as they got to the Joseph Smith story, they flipped the page over to the portrait of the Prophet Joseph Smith; and she said, "That is the man." She also is in the Church.

Of course, not all conversions are that spectacular. And not all spiritual promptings are listened to immediately. There was a Baptist couple down in Corpus Christi who were really active in their own church; but they let the missionaries teach them the discussions. When the missionaries got to the point where they presented the baptismal challenge, the couple said, "We've decided to stay active in our own church." Yet all through the lessons they had committed and known the teachings they had heard were true. Still, right at the last, they again said, "No, we are going to go back to our own church." The husband was teaching Sunday School. The wife also had a position in their Baptist congregation, and their two boys were active.

This couple later said that a month passed and their church

attendance declined. After six months they were totally inactive. Finally, after almost a year, the wife approached her husband and asked, "Don't you think we'd better go back to church?"

He asked, "Which one?"

She answered, "The Mormon Church."

He said, "Yes, we'd better." And they came over to church. I was there the night that this couple and their two children were baptized.

You see, it is very difficult for people to come into the Church when all of their roots are elsewhere. They get a testimony and they know they have heard the truth; but can you imagine what a traumatic experience it is to lose all of your friends and leave behind all those who despise the LDS Church and are so critical?

Sometimes you don't know exactly what is holding up the commitment. I was at the mission office one day, and Elder Gifford, who was a zone leader, called me up and said, "President, we are working with a Lutheran minister. He let us teach him. We had him on his knees, and he prayed with us and asked if the Church was true; but we can't get him to commit. He must have some questions. Would you mind coming out and talking to him?"

I said, "No, I'd be delighted to. Does he know I'm coming?"

Elder Gifford responded, "Oh, no. We didn't dare tell him you were coming until we had found out whether or not you could come."

I said, "You go ask him; and if he'll let me come, I'd be glad to come."

They called back and told me that he had said that a visit would be all right. So I went to Knippa, Texas, with Elder Gifford on Friday about 2:00 P.M. He was actually a former Lutheran minister and had moved over into the Knippa area in Texas and, as I recall, had bought about fifty acres and was just living off the land. He had a few cattle, some bees, a garden, and so forth. He had let his beard grow; and he and his family were really living modestly by our standards. They were eating well and doing most things well; but they lived humbly. They welcomed us into their home, which he had built. It had rough-hewn floorboards. It was rustic throughout, but really nice and clean.

Elder Gifford asked if we could have a prayer. They agreed, so we did. Then Elder Gifford said, "We've asked President Featherstone to answer any questions you may have." I told him who I was and what my assignment was as a mission president. Then I told him I was also a member of the First Quorum of the Seventy. Because of his scriptural background he had an interest in that.

After about ten minutes, I said, "Please feel free to ask any question you would like about the Church."

He said, "I don't have any questions."

That really surprised me. I felt a need to say something lest we all find ourselves sitting there in silence. So I started telling him what the usual questions were and gave him the full answers. I went through about six of the hard ones — from polygamy to tithing. Then, again, I said, "Now, do you have any questions?"

He said, "No." So I went through some more of the standard questions. It was almost like an interview with myself. Of course, I meant it to be a sort of interview with him.

Then I said, "Any other questions?"

By now about forty minutes had passed and he said, "Well, yes, I do have one." He opened his Doctrine and Covenants and read just a little quote and asked a very simple question. I think he just wanted to make sure he had asked a question so that I wouldn't feel bad about him not asking any questions. I answered that one and said, "Any more?"

He said, "No."

I said, "Well, Brother Joens, normally when we come to a home we really love to kneel with the family and have a prayer. We'd like to do that. Again, normally it would be up to you to decide who should pray; but would you mind if I would give the prayer today? I feel impressed to, and I would really like to leave a blessing in your home if that is all right with you."

He said, "I'd like you to do that."

So we knelt down, all of us—his family, the two missionaries, and myself—and had a prayer. When we got up off our knees, Brother Joens came over to me and said, "Last Monday when the elders were here they challenged me to be baptized. I asked the Lord if I should. While I was praying I had a very strong impression that before I would be baptized the president would come to my home and offer a prayer in my home. That has been done. I'd like to be baptized."

They baptized him the following Monday in a little creek that flows through his property. They dammed it up and baptized him and his family in that little pond.

There is an awakening, as President Kimball calls it, a brooding of the Spirit. Who knows how many thousands—even hundreds of thousands—are out there waiting for a knock on the door? Wouldn't it be a marvelous thing if, instead of near 30 percent, we could send 80 or 90 percent of our young men on missions? Commitment is the word—commitment in families, commitment from childhood on, commitment to go, and commitment to prepare. Often there is commitment, but to the wrong goals first. There has to be a changing of priorities. And if there were, strangely enough, the other commitments would more likely be fulfilled in the right order and for the right purposes.

I would like to share a few excerpts from *Ben Hur*. They are in my book *A Generation of Excellence*, but they seem to be especially applicable here. It is a great example of commitment.

In a memorable quotation from Lew Wallace's great book, a father, Simonides, describes his daughter: "The Lord hath been good to me in many ways; but thou, Esther, art the sovereign excellence of his favor." A young woman reading this may well find a goal for which she would work. For her father, her bishop, or for someone she prized to say such a thing about her would indeed be a strong motivational factor in her life.

The *spirit* of greatness comes out loud and clear as Simonides, who is responsible for all investments of the Hur family, questions Malluch the servant concerning Ben Hur.

> "In what he said or did, Malluch, could you in anywise detect his master-idea?" [Meaning, his main motive for his words and actions.]
> "As to that, Master Simonides," Malluch responds, "I can answer with much assurance. He is devoted to finding his mother and sister — that first. Then he has a grievance against Rome; and as the Messala of whom I told you had something to do with the wrong, the great present object is to humiliate him. . . ."
> "The Messala is influential," said Simonides, thoughtfully.
> "Yes; but the next meeting will be in the Circus."
> "Well, and then?"
> "The son of Arrius [Ben Hur] will win."
> "How know you?"
> Malluch smiled.
> "I am judging by what he says."
> "Is that all?"
> "No; there is a much better sign — his spirit."
> "Ay; but Malluch, his idea of vengeance — what is its scope? . . . Is his feeling but the vagary of a sensitive boy, or has it the seasoning of suffering manhood to give it endurance?"

Many of us who have worked with young men and women have found youth with great spirit. It's more than what they say, it's a spirit that thunders so loudly that no one can misunderstand.

Recall again with me the words of Ben Hur as he met with Sheik Ilderim and discussed the possibility of riding the sheik's four Arabian white stallions in the circus against Messala:

> "Enough!" he said. "If at the roots of thy tongue is a lie in coil, Solomon himself had not been safe against thee. . . . But as to thy skill. What experience hast thou in racing with chariots? And the horses — canst thou make them creatures of thy will . . . to come at call? To go, if thou sayest it, to the last extreme of breath and strength? . . . The gift, my son, is not to everyone. Ah . . . I knew a king who governed millions of men, their perfect master, but could not win the respect of a horse."

And then Ben Hur's response:

"I know now why it is that in the love of an Arab his horse is next to his children; and I know, also, why the Arab horses are the best in the world; but, good sheik, I would not have you judge me by words alone; for, as you know, all promises of men sometimes fail. Give me the trial first on some plain hereabout, and put the four in my hand tomorrow. . . . I tell thee thy sons of the Desert, though they have separately the speed of eagles and the endurance of lions, will fail if they are not trained to run together under the yoke. For bethink thee, Sheik, in every four there is one the slowest and one the swiftest."

Then came the competition between Ben Hur and the four Arabians of Sheik Ilderim against Messala. Before the eyes of the excited crowd, with the chariots side by side, with lightning quickness Messala reached out and whipped the flesh of the white Arabians that had never to that day felt the whip. But the hardening experience of the galleys gave Ben Hur the ascendancy over even that emergency. "So he kept his place, and gave the four free rein, and called to them in soothing voice, trying merely to guide them round the dangerous turn; and before the fever of the people began to abate, he had back the mastery [and] the sympathy and admiration of every one not a Roman." Ben Hur won the race — the direct result of his *character* as an individual.

I have always loved the poem that follows. I have committed it to memory. It is called "The Fool's Prayer," and was written by Edward R. Sill.

> The royal feast was done; the King
>   Sought some new sport to banish care,
> And to his jester cried: "Sir Fool,
>   Kneel now, and make for us a prayer!"
>
> The jester doffed his cap and bells,
>   And stood the mocking court before;
> They could not see the bitter smile
>   Behind the painted grin he wore.
>
> He bowed his head, and bent his knee
>   Upon the monarch's silken stool;
> His pleading voice arose: "O Lord,
>   Be merciful to me, a fool!
>
> "No pity, Lord, could change the heart

From red with wrong to white as wool;
The rod must heal the sin: but, Lord,
Be merciful to me, a fool!

" 'Tis not by guilt the onward sweep
Of truth and right, O Lord, we stay;
'Tis by our follies that so long
We hold the earth from heaven away.

"These clumsy feet, still in the mire,
Go crushing blossoms without end;
These hard, well-meaning hands we thrust
Among the heart-strings of a friend.

"The ill-timed truth we might have kept —
Who knows how sharp it pierced and stung?
The word we had not sense to say —
Who knows how grandly it had rung?

"Our faults no tenderness should ask,
The chastening stripes must cleanse them all;
But for our blunders — Oh, in shame
Before the eyes of heaven we fall.

"Earth bears no balsam for mistakes;
Men crown the knave, and scourge the tool
That did his will; but Thou, O Lord,
Be merciful to me, a fool!"

The room was hushed; in silence rose
The King, and sought his gardens cool,
And walked apart, and murmured low,
"Be merciful to me, a fool!"

(*One Hundred and One Famous Poems*, pages 159-160.)

Even a king can change or modify a commitment. Some would call this repentance. Our greatest loyalty, our greatest allegiance, must be to our Savior. Every soul should keep sacred the commitments that are true and eternal, such as faithfulness to our husbands and wives, honest toil for our employer, self-development and improvement principles, and love for the Savior. There is no conflict between good and true commitments; so if you feel conflict, seek for the errant commitment, the one that wanders from the core of truth that is in Christ. Then discard it. That is what wisdom dictates.

7

Love of Christ Ties
All Commitments Together

Throughout this book I have kept coming back to the idea that all commitments should be based on a commitment to our Savior. Otherwise our commitments may not be harmonious: They may work against each other. For instance, it would be impossible to have a commitment to eventually arrive in the celestial kingdom and at the same time be firmly resolved to be the world's greatest hit man or the world's highest-paid burlesque entertainer. Satan is served by sin; but God is served by love and righteousness. We show which one we love by our commitments.

Of course, we are all developing and maturing, as in our taste in music. You usually don't arrive at the stage where you love most the words of David and Isaiah and the music of Handel and Beethoven and others who were inspired by David and Isaiah very early in life. You probably will be a Rodgers and Hammerstein addict before that. And still earlier, perhaps, you may have a passion for Elton John or even the Beatles. And, of course, you will never give up loving the best of the worlds of jazz and rock, because they do produce some beautiful music. But these are lesser stars in the heavens of music. They do not shine as brightly as those that reflect the shining light of the bright and morning star. (Revelation 22:16.)

I am trying to appeal to your innate desire to grow. I had an experience with one of my sons which might help me explain, at least in part, the point I am getting at. This happened a number of years ago. Our son Lawrence had promised to get tickets to an Elton John concert for his brother Scott. Perhaps this story will go over better if I explain that I like some of Elton John's music. We had a lot of his records in our home. Scott played the piano, and I had to listen to him playing Elton John music. So I heard a lot of Elton John.

Scott had one of those shirts with *Elton John* embroidered across the back. I said, "Scott, you have a good name. Why don't you have *Scott Featherstone* embroidered across the back?" But I guess that wasn't a very good idea.

I came back from a stake conference visit one night about 11 P.M. and Lawrence said, "Dad, would you take me up to the University of Utah tomorrow morning?"

I said, "What for?"

He responded, "Scott called and he wants me to get some Elton John tickets for him."

"What time do we have to get up there? What time does the box office open?"

Lawrence said, "About 9 A.M., I believe."

I said, "Well, if we get up there by 7 A.M., would that be early enough?"

He said, "Dad! We've got to be up there by 5 A.M."

Events proved that Lawrence and I didn't fully grasp the Elton John situation. We got up at 4:30 A.M. and drove up to the Special Events Center. You can't believe the mass of humanity we found. I told Lawrence it would take him two days to find the end of the line. This was a Monday morning, you understand. We learned that the first people got in line Friday afternoon, and the line had been growing ever since. Talk about feeling like the last one to dinner!

When Lawrence and I faced the day of reckoning, I said to

Scott, "Suppose you had never seen or heard the prophet in your whole life, would you stand outside the Tabernacle doors from Friday to Monday to get a ticket to go to conference?" That had never entered his mind. I am amazed at the motivation of young people. I am also amazed at the misdirection that motivation sometimes takes. But I suppose it is not until we have been totally immersed in the glory and mercy of the Savior that the great Christian composers of word and song really sound better than the music of rock and jazz. I don't know the source of the inspiration of some of our current musicians and poets; but I know that the great Christian composers were students of Job, David, Isaiah, and other great biblical artists whose inspiration was all centered in Christ. I love the following statement from Adam Clarke:

> But the highest merit of David, and that which seems to have been almost exclusively *his own*, was his *poetic genius*. As a Divine poet, even God himself had created none greater, either *before* or *since*. In this science and gift he is therefore the [masterpiece] of the Almighty. *Moses* wrote some fine verses; *Solomon* two fine poems, an *ode* and an *elegy*. The prophets, particularly *Isaiah*, in several *chapters* of his prophecy; *Jeremiah*, in his book of *Lamentations;* and some of the *minor prophets*, in a few *select verses*, have given us specimens of a profound poetical genius; but we have no *whole* like that of David. The *sublimity*, the *depth*, the *excursive fancy*, the *discursive power*, the *vast compass* of *thought*, the knowledge of *heaven* and *earth*, of *God* and *nature*, the work of the Spirit, the endlessly varied temptations of Satan, the knowledge of the human heart, the travail of the soul, the full comprehension of the . . . *personification* of the whole of *inanimate nature*, of every *virtue*, and of every *vice*, the immense grasp of thought embodying and arranging, and afterwards clothing in suitable language, the vast assemblage of ideas furnished by the natural and spiritual world; in a word, the spirit of poetry, the true *genie createur*, the . . . *framework of the framer*, the *poetry of the poet*, not the *fiction* of the *inventive* genius; but the production of truth, hidden before in the bosom of God and nature, and exhibited in the most pleasing colours, with the most impressive pathos and irresistible harmonic diction: these qualities, these supramundane excellences, are found in no other poet that ever graced the annals of the world; they exist in their perfection only in David king of Israel. What is peculiarly remarkable in David is,

he has succeeded to the very highest degree in every species of poetic composition that has for its *object* the glory of God and the welfare of man; and there is not one poet who has succeeded him, that has not failed when he attempted to sing of God, the punishment and rewards of the future world, and the unsearchable riches of Christ.

The *hymns* which he produced have been the general song of the universal Church; and men of all nations find in these compositions a language at once suitable to their feelings, and expressive of their highest joys and deepest sorrows, as well as of all the endlessly varied wishes and desires of their hearts. Hail, thou sweet singer of Israel! thy voice is still heard in all the assemblies of the saints. (*Clarke's Commentary*, Job to Malachi, pages 696-7. Italics as in original.)

The sentiments and very words of David truly do still ring in the assemblies of the Saints—the Latter-day Saints. Read again Psalms 22 through 25 and see how many of the greatest of hymns you can name that have taken words and concepts from these poetic utterances. The main point I wish to make in quoting Clarke on David is that the Messiah, whom we call Jesus, was the inspiration of David. To him David prayed. Of him he sang. About him he composed over a hundred hymns of the most excellent and even prophetic quality (though it is not easy to prove that many really were about Jesus). In any event, they carry his Spirit and speak his words. All David's hope for ultimate pardon rested in his Messiah. Indeed, it is no exaggeration to say that David's psalms were the psalms of Jesus; for the Saints can speak from the mind of Christ. (1 Corinthians 2:16.) He is the Shepherd, the Stone of Israel (Matthew 21:42-44), the sure foundation whereon if men build, they cannot fall. (Acts 4:11-12; Helaman 5:12.) So the first task is to find the kingdom and take possession of the mind of Christ, which, as Paul explained to the Corinthians, is the legacy of the Saints.

Think what a contribution selfish people of great talent could have made if their commitments had been made to Jesus Christ instead of to themselves! We will do better in every aspect of our lives if we commit to a God in whose life we see miracles, power over disease and death; one who, as a glorified, resurrected being, said to John, his beloved disciple, "I am he that liveth, and was dead; and, behold, I am alive for evermore, Amen; and have the keys of hell and of death." (Revelation 1:18.)

Commit to no one less than this. Whose life says this much? Who else could truly say, "Come and follow me"? And where else can you truly follow him but in a church that bears his name and claims all the powers that he gave his disciples in antiquity when he was here on the earth? All who claim to be Christians should prayerfully exclaim: "Would God that it were true!"

To the Jew and to the Gentile of every nation, kindred, tongue, and people, I would like to declare my testimony of Jesus Christ by sharing some of the feelings in my heart as I have searched for my Messiah. In attempting to share with you my feelings about Jesus Christ, I am in no way trying to prove to you his divinity. I am sharing my innermost feelings of why I love him so much and why he has been able to enlist me body and soul into his cause.

As a boy of nine or ten I purchased a paperback copy of a Bible for twenty-five cents. Reading about Abraham and his intercession on behalf of the people of Sodom, I felt a warmth in my soul. I am sure that my cheeks flushed and my heart expanded as I read how Abraham entreated the Lord to spare the city if there were fifty righteous souls, then forty-five, forty, thirty, twenty, and finally ten. The love the Lord had for his servant Abraham and the respect he had for even ten righteous souls would have saved Sodom if there had been ten righteous souls there. I learned later that Abraham followed and worshipped Christ just as we follow and worship Christ. There was nothing primitive about his religion.

As a young man I read with intense interest the account of Moses as he led the flock to the backside of the desert and came to the mountain of God, even to Horeb.

> And the angel of the Lord appeared unto him in a flame of fire out of the midst of a bush: and he looked, and, behold, the bush burned with fire, and the bush was not consumed.

> And Moses said, I will not turn aside, and see this great sight, why the bush is not burnt.
>
> And when the Lord saw that he turned aside to see, God called unto him out of the midst of the bush, and said, Moses, Moses. And he said, Here am I.
>
> And he said, Draw not nigh hither: put off thy shoes from off thy feet, for the place whereon thou standest is holy ground.
>
> Moreover he said, I am the God of thy father, the God of Abraham, the God of Isaac, and the God of Jacob. And Moses hid his face; for he was afraid to look upon God. (Exodus 3:2-6.)

I felt like I was living with Moses. In my young imagination I could see these things transpire. My love of the God of ancient Israel was increased through the awe and reverence I felt for the great men who sought him and loved him.

Later in my life the scriptures became a constant companion. I have read from them daily for the last thirty years of my life. The vicarious experiences I have had could not be bought with all the treasures of the earth. I have associated with many of the great and noble of the earth. I have felt like Elisha must have felt when he was with Elijah just prior to Elijah's ascension to heaven in a whirlwind.

> And Elijah took his mantle, and wrapped it together, and smote the waters, and they were divided hither and thither, so that they two went over on dry ground.
>
> And it came to pass, when they were gone over, that Elijah said unto Elisha, Ask what I shall do for thee, before I be taken away from thee. And Elisha said, I pray thee, let a double portion of thy spirit be upon me. (2 Kings 2:8-9.)

I have often felt to say, "Let a double portion of thy spirit rest upon me" as I have associated with the Brethren and have come to know and love them. The best men and the greatest men I know have committed their lives and souls to Jesus Christ.

I remember the feelings I had when I read the account of the woman who had an issue of blood for twelve years. The scriptures say that she had spent all her living upon physicians, neither could be healed of any. How often we find souls in the same situation today! Reference to having spent all her living would lead us to believe she was in dire and desperate circumstances "and was nothing bettered, but rather grew worse." We see those who suffer for years from disease and sickness; and who of us is not moved with great compassion and feels his utter helplessness in relieving the suffering ones? For twelve long years, 4,383 days, the woman had suffered. Now she had heard of Jesus and his miracles; and as Jesus went and much people with him and thronged about him, this woman said, "If I may touch but his clothes, I shall be whole." She came in the "press" of the crowd behind Jesus and touched his garment "and straight-way the fountain of her blood was dried up; and she felt in her body that she was healed of that plague." Apparently she then fell back through the crowd, the miracle complete. Her bosom must have swelled with inexpressible gratitude.

"And Jesus, immediately knowing in himself that virtue had gone out of him, turned him about in the press, and said, Who touched my clothes?" The disciples must have been shocked at this question, for they responded, "Thou seest the multitude thronging thee, and sayest thou, Who touched me?"

Jesus "looked round about to see her that had done this thing." Now note the woman's attitude. This poor, gentle, healed one, fearing and trembling, knowing what was done in her, came and fell down before him; and stripped of all false pride and in pure humility, possibly even feeling guilty for this act, told him the whole truth. We can see her kneeling before the Savior with tear-filled eyes, totally and absolutely submissive to his will.

Then we hear this from our beloved Lord: "Daughter, thy faith hath made thee whole; go in peace, and be whole of thy plague." (Mark 5:25-34.) The initial healing was through her faith. His blessing was a ratification which confirmed her faith. She was whole. To me this incident is one of the most beautiful in all the scriptures to show the magnificent love of Jesus Christ. I felt his compassion and love toward others, and my love increased toward him.

Again, in a very special way, another scriptural account of my Messiah taught me an important lesson of life. He and his disciples "went thence, and departed into the coasts of Tyre and Sidon. And, behold, a woman of Canaan came out of the same coasts." She also must have had some knowledge about his miracles. The meeting was not by chance. She sought him. When she found him, she "cried unto him, saying, . . . O lord, thou Son of David; my daughter is grievously vexed with a devil." There is no question that he heard her, "but he answered her not a word." The woman for herself may not have pressed the issue further; but for the love for her daughter, she continued to pursue her request. The disciples, noting that he had ignored her request and given her no heed, "came and besought him, saying, Send her away; for she crieth after us." I cannot believe that any of our Brethren today would do that.

The Savior still did not respond to the woman, but to his disciples he said, "I am not sent but unto the lost sheep of the house of Israel." The disciples apparently had to ponder his response, but the woman impulsively came and worshipped him, saying, simply "Lord, help me."

A person would have to be made of stone to ignore this pitiful plea. In my mind I can picture her kneeling before him, pleading with her eyes as well as her voice, "Lord, help me!" To this desperate request the Lord gave this, to our age, incredible reply, "It is not meet to take the children's bread, and to cast it to dogs." The woman kneeling in front of him could have stood up and said, "I am not a dog, I do not have to be insulted like that. I have some pride, too, you know." She did not. In one of the greatest expressions of love and humility, forgetting self, again stripping away all false pride, she said, "Truth, Lord: yet the dogs eat of the crumbs which fall from their masters' table."

"Then Jesus answered and said unto her, O woman, great is thy faith: be it unto thee even as thou wilt. And her daughter was made whole from that very hour." (Matthew 15:21-28.)

It took much thought and prayer to understand this experience. I couldn't imagine the Master I worship with all my heart appearing to be so harsh. Understanding came. Of course he was emphasizing the covenant with Israel, that all nations were to be blessed through Israel, and Israel through the Messiah. In the wisdom of God, the gospel would be first taken to the Jews, and Jesus' ministry was to be with them. (2 Nephi 10:3-5.) Also, he undoubtedly knew the heart of this woman; and during the moments she pled with him and he did not respond, I'm sure he could discern her spirit and knew what her responses would be. It was a great teaching moment, not only for his disciples, but for all generations of man from that time forth. The lesson this noble woman taught us about humility and trust in absolute acceptance of the order of God's kingdom will be a blessing to us forever. As we read her beautiful, humble response, suddenly we have a vision of what true humility is and how it must please our Lord. I am so grateful that some translator did not leave this account out, feeling it was unworthy of Jesus. Many of us never would have had one of the supreme lessons in humility in all of the writings of the Savior. I love him for his love and ability to teach with impact. This lesson was for Jesus' disciples as well as for the woman and the crowd.

Again I saw the Messiah as he "went into a city called Nain; and many of his disciples went with him, and much people." He didn't rebuke the crowds or send them away. He understood their need. This day as they flocked after him, "he came nigh to the gate of the city." There he beheld "a dead man carried out, the only son of his mother, and she was a widow." The throng following Jesus must have stopped as he stopped to behold the funeral procession.

On this occasion conditions were different. We find that Jesus was viewing something of which he was not a part. Those in the procession probably did not take notice of him as he stood and watched the procession "with much people." The young man was dead and had been laid on a bier which was being carried through the streets of the city. The widowed mother was grief stricken. The large crowd that attended the funeral procession was probably an indication of the sympathy which the people of the city felt for this widow's loss of her only son. I imagine that, as she followed those carrying the bier, she walked with her head bowed, suffering a grief that was beyond description.

The Master approached her and "had compassion on her, and said unto her, Weep not." She must have looked up to see who thus addressed her. I can visualize her swollen, tired eyes looking into his, and the words she had heard seeming to be spoken by one who truly did care and who could feel every bit of her suffering. This brief confrontation with the widow and what transpired as he looked into her soul and said, "Weep not," can only be imagined. Then "he came and touched the bier: and they that bare him stood still. And he said, Young man, I say unto thee, Arise. And he that was dead sat up, and began to speak. And he delivered the boy to his mother." (Luke 7:11-17.)

I think as Jesus performed this miracle his heart must have been full, for he knew in an incomprehensible way the joy that would come to the widowed mother in the next few moments. Had we been there, we probably would have seen him shed tears of love. I wonder if he didn't stand there for just a moment or two, feeling, as none of us can, the overflowing joy of a widow's heart as she clung fiercely to her son.

I love Jesus for his love. I love him for his gentleness, his mercy, his forgiving heart. I love him for his long-suffering, for his absolute purity and his charity. I love him as my Savior and Redeemer, the great I Am, the King of kings. And I worship him because he is literally the Son of God.

I would like now to shift to some of the glorious modern revelations which have come from my Messiah. He loves us and speaks to us today, too. He is still the Messiah and he operates the same as he did in the days of Abraham, Moses, and Elijah, and the same as he did when he came in the meridian of time when he was rejected by the Jews. At a special conference held at Hiram, Ohio, November 1, 1831, the Lord revealed a proclamation of warning and commandment to the Church and to the inhabitants of the earth. A few verses follow:

> And the voice of warning shall be unto all people, by the mouths of my disciples, whom I have chosen in these last days.

> And they shall go forth and none shall stay them, for I the Lord have commanded them.
>
> Behold, this is mine authority, and the authority of my servants, and my preface unto the book of my commandments, which I have given them to publish unto you, O inhabitants of the earth.
>
> Wherefore, fear and tremble, O ye people, for what I the Lord have decreed in them shall be fulfilled.
>
> And verily I say unto you, that they who go forth, bearing these tidings unto the inhabitants of the earth, to them is power given to seal both on earth and in heaven, the unbelieving and rebellious; . . .
>
> And also those to whom these commandments were given, might have power to lay the foundation of this church, and to bring it forth out of obscurity and out of darkness, the only true and living church upon the face of the whole earth, with which I the Lord, am well pleased. (D&C 1:4-8, 30.)

The faithful members of the Church of Jesus Christ bear their solemn and sacred witness that Jesus Christ has visited the earth in our day, that he has once again established his church on the earth. We know, as did certain devout Jews of every nation on the day of Pentecost, that Jesus who was crucified was both Lord and Christ. Ours is not a belief nor a hope, not a feeling nor a tradition. It is purely and simply a knowledge and a witness that there is only one authorized agency on the face of the earth that has the keys, gifts, and power to function as the Church of Jesus Christ. We have a special witness which we bear to Jew and Gentile alike to come unto Christ. Be not faithless but believing.

To the Jews we declare, "Come and find the Messiah whom ye seek. Peter, Paul, James, and John and other Jews have added to their ancient witness a modern witness that Jesus Christ is the Messiah whom ye seek. Humble yourselves before the great God of heaven and receive your personal witness. His arms are outstretched to you, his beloved chosen people. His love extends mercy and blessing to all who will come unto him. We plead with you, O Israel, give ear to him who 'would have gathered you under his wings as a hen gathereth her chickens and ye would not.' We bear witness that the time will soon come when all Israel will know. Exercise your faith and look not further for a Messiah. For he has come. Come into the true fold of Christ and be numbered among his sheep, that you may once again know the true shepherd who laid down his life for his sheep. His words are true and faithful and they will come to pass. In this day in a revelation the Savior revealed to the Prophet Joseph those things that will transpire before your brethren will accept the gospel as a nation."

Then shall the arm of the Lord fall upon the nations.

And then shall the Lord set his foot upon this mount, and it shall cleave in twain, and the earth shall tremble, and reel to and fro, and the heavens also shall shake.

And the Lord shall utter his voice, and all the ends of the earth shall hear it; and the nations of the earth shall mourn, and they that have laughed shall see their folly.

And calamity shall cover the mocker, and the scorner shall be consumed; and they that have watched for iniquity shall be hewn down and cast into the fire.

And then shall the Jews look upon me and say: What are these wounds in thine hands and in thy feet?

Then shall they know that I am the Lord; for I will say unto them: These wounds are the wounds with which I was wounded in the house of my friends. I am he who was lifted up. I am Jesus that was crucified. I am the Son of God.

And then shall they weep because of their iniquities; then shall they lament because they persecuted their king. (D&C 45:47-53.)

O House of Judah, you can surely know. Do not delay your investigation of The Church of Jesus Christ of Latter-day Saints one more hour. The Lord said, "My sheep hear my voice." (John 10:3-16.) You will have a special witness as you read the New Testament, which is a witness for Jesus Christ. You will read the Book of Mormon, which is a second witness for Christ; and you will have that sure knowledge that Jesus is Jehovah, the very Messiah. Yea, then you will rejoice because you will have walked by faith and will not have waited to be converted with your nation when that time comes when all Israel will know in sorrow.

We declare our love for you Gentiles. Come and be grafted into the true vine. Join yourself and kindred to modern Israel.

There is a God in heaven who lives. He is a personal God. He is literally the Father of Jesus Christ. Jesus is the Only Begotten of the Father in the flesh. God the Father and Jesus Christ have visited the earth again in this day. Peter, James, and John have restored the apostolic authority which gave Joseph Smith the authorization to organize Christ's Church. The Church is named after Jesus Christ because it is his Church. It has a prophet who stands at the head of the Church who is just a whisper away from the Savior. He receives revelation and inspiration to guide the Church in these troubled times. There is a quorum of twelve living apostles who hold the same keys and authorities which the ancient apostles held. The priesthood and its power have been conferred upon worthy men so that the kingdom can function. Every priesthood bearer in the Church can trace his priesthood authority back to Jesus Christ.

God the Father and Jesus Christ are not mysterious essences, or ethereal substances without form, which fill the immensity of space while dwelling in the souls of men. They are not part of a trinity that is of one substance that is a nonsubstance with three distinct manifestations, the Father, the Son, and the Holy Ghost, the so-called Triune God.

We know by special witness of modern prophets who actually saw them that they are separate and distinct personages. We know that the Father and the Son have bodies of flesh and bone as tangible as man's, but the Holy Ghost is a personage of spirit. Remember the words of the Ten Commandments which have thundered down from Sinai: "Thou shalt have no other gods before me."

Come to a church which tithes its members. As the Prophet Joseph said, a church that does not have the power to call upon its members to sacrifice everything does not have the power to save them. Come and pay your tithes and offerings; and, as the Lord has promised, he will open up the windows of heaven and pour out a blessing that you have not room to receive. (Malachi 3:8-10.)

Jesus had the power to seal on earth and in heaven. Again men have been given those sealing powers. They are sacred powers and they are used to seal a man and his wife and children together as a family unit for all eternity. These sealing powers are found only in this Church. Others may claim to have these powers; but we testify boldly and humbly that they are counterfeit powers and avail nothing. All of the hosts of your ancestors who died without an opportunity to hear the gospel and embrace its truth will yet have that privilege. This is the reason that the Savior has directed that we seek after our dead. Proxy work is done in the temples to provide a means of eternal exaltation for all mankind. Free agency is an eternal principle and ever and always will be exercised. The dead for whom the proxy work is done will still have the right to accept or reject the work that is done for them. The gospel will be preached to them in the spirit world.

The Savior's Church was a proselyting church. The world can hardly comprehend the great ends to which the Church goes to see that every living soul has an opportunity to hear the gospel of Jesus Christ. Great hosts of missionaries and members, constantly, with the patience and persistence of fishers and hunters, attempt to share the gospel with friends and neighbors.

Again, we invite all to come and participate, to contribute their work and talents to the great welfare program of the Church of Jesus Christ. Welfare in the Church of Jesus Christ is motivated by charity, which is the pure love of Christ. In the Savior's welfare program we contribute time, talents, and monies for the benefit of all. The poor, the widow, the afflicted, the jobless—all come under the great umbrella of charity in the Church. Each soul who receives maintains dignity and self-respect because each works to the extent of his or her ability for that which is received.

There is an organization which we call the Primary for children who are ages three to eleven. Remember the Savior said, "Suffer the little children to come unto me." The Savior's organization for women, the great Relief Society, draws all women together in a Christlike sisterhood. The aged, the youth, the young adult, the widow, the widower, the handicapped and disadvantaged, the rich and poor, the executive and laborer, the doctor, the teacher, the student, and every living soul find meaning and refuge in the Church. Why? Because it is Christ's true Church.

I once heard president Harold B. Lee quote Abraham Lincoln in about these words: If a man had a tightrope and stretched it across Niagara Falls, then he commenced to attempt to cross the tightrope, carrying in his arms everything you treasured as priceless and dear, you would not be yelling at him trying to get him to lose his balance and fall. You would be kneeling and praying with all of your soul that he would make it. So it is with The Church of Jesus Christ of Latter-day Saints. Every soul on the earth who has heard the message ought to kneel and pray with all his or her heart that it is true. They ought to say, "Would to God that it were true."

It would seem that everyone would want a church which declares that Jesus Christ has personally visited the earth and reestablished his Church. Indeed, shouldn't every person desire to have a church which is led by God's living oracles, modern apostles and prophets, a church that has sealing powers which are used to seal a family together for all eternity? "Would to God that it were true."

Again to the Jew and to the Gentile, we invite you to come and see. We have found the Messiah. Indeed, Jesus is the Christ, the Son of the living God. He is the great I Am, the Redeemer, our Lord of lords, our King of kings, our Savior and God. The Church of Jesus Christ of Latter-day Saints is his true and living Church. All our commitments should be centered in him. As Helaman 5:12 indicates, he is the "sure foundation, a foundation whereon if men build they cannot fall."